As If We Were There

Readings for
a Transformative
Passover Experience

RABBI GIDON ROTHSTEIN

KODESH PRESS

As If We Were There: Readings for
a Transformative Passover Experience
© Gidon Rothstein 2016

ISBN: 978-0692635681

Cover image "Parting of the Red Sea"
Jose Vega - Illustrator
www.josevega.carbonmade.com
Image used by permission

The publisher extends its gratitude to Rabbi Yeshayahu Ginsburg for his help with this project.

Published & Distributed by
Kodesh Press L.L.C.
New York, NY
www.KodeshPress.com
kodeshpress@gmail.com

TABLE OF CONTENTS

PART I

As If We Were There

Rosh Chodesh Nisan

Introduction:
The Challenge and the Way to Meet It

Just about at the end of our telling the story on Seder night, we find out that there has been an agenda to the evening we might have missed up until that point. After all the telling we've done, we quote Mishnah *Pesachim* 10:5, that in every generation we are to see ourselves as if we left Egypt. As Deut. 6:21-25 reports the story, we are to tell our children when they ask about the commandments of Seder night, verse 23 has us saying "and us He took out of there," which Rava in *Pesachim* 116b sees as an obligation.

It's not enough to retell the events, to bring our children into the circle of those who know a long-ago story; when each of us says to our children (as Exod.13:14 commands us) that it was for this service that God took *me* out of Egypt, we are supposed to mean that as close to literally as we can get.

The goal is to *relive* the events, to walk away from our Seder having rejuvenated our sense of the Exodus as a personal experience, not a piece of history. A completely successful Seder night would bring its participants to the *Hallel*, the Psalms of praise recited both before and after the meal, and to the meal itself, as jubilant as those who physically experienced the Exodus itself.

That's a tall order, and I cannot say I know how to achieve it. I do believe that this book will help us get closer to that goal, in two parts. The first part comes in 21 pieces, one for each day from the first of Nisan through the end of Pesach. I believe that if you join me in reading those, one entry a day, you will feel that we have made good progress on this one narrow goal: having our Seder turn the past into the present, enabling us to say, meaning it almost literally, "and us He took from there."

The second part of this book comes in sixteen pieces; it can be read in conjunction with this part, also suitable for one-a-day reading from the beginning of Nisan through the first days of the holiday, or before. It is a memoir of my father's Seder, which I hope offers a model to build our own Sedarim. But more on that when we get to it.

Putting Ourselves Back in Egypt

I start with the recognition that for all that we talk as if we tell the story of leaving Egypt Seder night, we don't do that much of it. We offer several concise versions, the longest of which is four verses, whose key terms we then explain at length.

We could have spent the night on the first chapters of the book of Exodus, guided by the voluminous commentarial literature, which turns the Exodus from a cardboard cartoon into a textured drama, populated by relatable human beings. Except that that's a lot to read, let alone discuss or analyze.

It's also my personal experience that the flow of the Seder doesn't really allow for study of lengthy comments printed underneath the text of the Haggadah.

It's not clear we could do it even if we tried—those are rich chapters, and we have perhaps two hours of storytelling time at our Seder. It's one reason that preparation will help, a bit each day of this month of Nisan, until we reach the Seder.

Asking you to join me in a chapter by chapter review of the book of Exodus might not be so tempting, however—it's long, and it feels sort of familiar, since many of us have learned it before, or have heard it read. We want an approach that stimulates openness, so we can renew and relive the Exodus.

My attempt here is to adapt a technique some museums use to bring their stories alive. By focusing on the characters in the story, asking how they did, how we might have hoped to do better, we can begin to see ourselves in the story, to picture ourselves in Egypt. And then see ourselves leaving.

The key is realizing that some participants in the events leading up to the Exodus did better, some worse. The first step to that is brushing aside the pretense that Hashem controlled the events fully, with humans playing preordained and unchangeable roles. Traditional commentators—here, I use some of my personal favorites: R. Baruch haLevi Epstein's selections of Rabbinic literature in his *Torah Temimah*, Rashi, Ramban, R. Obadiah Sforno of sixteenth-century Italy, and *Kli Yakar* (Rabbi Shlomo Ephraim Luntschitz of the late 16th century/early 17th century Poland)—often frame the story so as to emphasize where humans did well or could have done better.

Join me, then, in two weeks of preparation for the Seder. Not the technicalities, important as those are, or even of reading the Haggadah, important as that is. Join me instead in a gradual immersion back in that time, so we can hit the end of the storytelling part of Seder night fully sincere in saying those crucial words, "and us He took from there."

Pesach All Year: *Mitzvot* that Keep Us in Mind of the Exodus

Once we reach the Seder, our work will not yet be done. Too often, we allow our retelling, or re-experiencing, to stop there. We go back to the rest of the year, limiting our encounters with the Exodus to the twice-daily mentions in the Shema, as well as Shabbat and the major holidays. It might seem that a Jew's regular life need not be continually engaged with the memory of *Yetziat Mitzrayim*, the Exodus from Egypt. Perhaps it is enough to bring it up occasionally, but not mention it with the frequency that we do.

Many Biblical commandments show that that's untrue, that the Exodus and Egypt are supposed to be part of the everyday fabric of ordinary Jewish lives. Once our daily readings have taken us through the Exodus story, we'll shift our attention to those commandments. Daily readings through the end of the holiday will review those commandments the Torah explicitly linked to our memory of the Exodus, enhancing our awareness of just how frequently Jews are supposed to relate their actions to their historical memory.

I focus on Biblical commandments because people too often dismiss Rabbinic rules as an external imposition of those rabbis' personal values on the Torah's "original" system. I reject that characterization, intellectually and viscerally, but by using Biblical ones, I can avoid the issue—the *mitzvot* we will study are all *Torah law*, part of the Torah's "original" intent for how Jews should live.

We are the people who left Egypt, a truth meant to inform many moments of each day. The memory of leaving Egypt is one of the aids the Torah gave us to bring that to fruition. Join me for the next three weeks, and I hope and believe we will find ourselves farther down the road to making that a reality.

We'll start tomorrow, asking ourselves whether we'd have understood what was happening as it unfolded.

Would We Have Seen Hashem in the Plagues?

The Torah emphasizes the supernatural in the Exodus, especially the plagues and the Splitting of the Sea. Hashem is quoted frequently to the effect that these wonders were to make clear to the Egyptians and the world Who was making this happen.

Taken at face value, it makes us wonder how the Egyptians denied the necessity of submitting to Hashem through ten full plagues and then, a few days later, decided to chase the Jews to the Sea. Why didn't they reconcile themselves to the inevitable?

Perhaps Hashem hardened Pharaoh's heart at some point, but that doesn't explain the conduct of the rest of the Egyptians, who did not urge him to let the Jews go until late in the game, and never forced him to do so. Their hearts weren't hardened, but they didn't respond as if it were completely clear that their only choice was to submit to Hashem.

Perhaps we can understand them better if we ask a different question: did the plagues obviously and undeniably come from Hashem? Some strands of tradition say no. Several commentators, especially Ramban but also Rashi, show how a stubborn denier could have convinced himself that the plagues were natural.

For them, the challenge wasn't to accept the blindingly obvious, it was to choose to acknowledge Hashem's orchestration of events, despite the possibility of explaining those events in some other way. (That also makes it more relevant to our lives, more comparable to challenges of faith today, where we have to choose the explanation that includes Hashem, even if there are other reasonable explanations).

Let's look at how Hashem left the Egyptians—and many Jews—room to misconstrue what was in front of them. And then to ask ourselves, what would we have done had we been there?

Replicable Plagues

When Aaron turns Egypt's waters to blood, Pharaoh's sorcerers do it as well. Rashi thinks Pharaoh concluded that Moses and Aaron were sorcerers, more powerful than his, but not essentially different. Once the plague fit a familiar framework, Pharaoh and his people could avoid changing their world view, and they could reject any need to grapple with whether this God was qualitatively different than other gods.

Drawing from *Chazal* (which goes without saying for Rashi, and henceforth will), Rashi also says that a week of plague was followed by three weeks of warnings. He likely thought this was to give the Egyptians time to learn the lessons of each plague, to react as they ought to have. But they could equally use it as breathing room, to let the memory of the plague fade, to reassure themselves nothing novel was happening, that life would continue as they were accustomed.

When introducing frogs (Exod. 7:27), Hashem speaks of being נֹגֵף, sending a plague. Rashi reads the verb as indicating a damaging but not completely destructive event. Today we might say the plagues were never an existential threat; they caused loss of property, displacement, discomfort, and occasional loss of life, but no realistic possibility of the Egyptians' losing their nation, their society, or their culture. The lower the threat level, the less they were forced to learn the lessons Hashem was teaching. And until they were forced, they found ways to avoid it.

Rashi's Lice: Beyond the Reach of the Natural

For Rashi, the sorcerers couldn't produce lice because the demons they used for their sorcery had no power over anything smaller than a barley-grain. In more modern terms, Rashi could be saying that there was (perhaps always is) a limit to humans' ability to control the world, through sorcery or science. Certain things, only Hashem can do.

The sorcerers recognize that Aaron cannot be the one manipulating something that small, that this is supernatural. They tell Pharaoh that the lice were not the work of mere sorcery. While they admit Aaron was doing something they could not, there was something self-serving in it, since they were saying no human could. Perhaps the stake they had in declaring Aaron to have superhuman powers is what helped Pharaoh reject their view.

They were right, but his reaction speaks to the difficulty we can have in accepting anything truly different. When would any of us accept that we had reached an absolute human limit, that there is no human way to accomplish some task?

The sorcerers correctly diagnosed events; Pharaoh shows the temptation to cling to our existing framework and the difficulty we have in knowing when we have to abandon it for a new one. Seeing Aaron as the most powerful sorcerer ever is still less disruptive or discomfiting than admitting Hashem's omnipotence.

Ramban's Lice: Supernatural How?

Ramban thinks the sorcerers generally *could* produce lice, and had done so on other occasions. Here, Hashem prevented them, which was how they knew this was the finger of God. His reading explains why they tried and failed to produce the lice. If they knew their magic didn't extend to lice, why try at all?

Ramban assumes the text stays silent about Hashem's intervention. His version also makes it even harder for non-sorcerers to see that this outcome was Hashem's direct actions, since they had seen sorcerers produce lice.

Without rejecting that, Ramban offers another idea, closer to Rashi's, noting that this plague was the first to create new material. The blood came from existing water, and the frogs were also already in existence (according to Ramban). The lice were new, however, and demons have no power to create something new.

This agrees with Rashi on how the sorcerers recognized Aaron's lice as supernatural, but differs on the bounds of the natural, in a way that also translates well to modern life. For Ramban, magic or science might be able to combine or transform existing substances remarkably, but truly new life will always beyond their capabilities.

Do we accept Ramban's distinction? Do we notice that modern science always builds off that which already exists? If we lose sight of that, we run the risk of emulating Pharaoh, deciding there is nothing in the plagues to induce us to rethink our worldview.

Gone, Not Forgotten

The sorcerers are not mentioned after lice until verse 9:11, when the Torah notes that they could not stand before Pharaoh when they were struck with boils. Ramban says their vulnerability embarrassed them so much that they locked themselves at home.

If so, they had still been at court for the intervening plagues; for all that they had conceded that the plagues were from Hashem, they clung to their respected position— Hashem and Aaron might be stronger, but they as sorcerers were still a power to be reckoned with, to be present as Pharaoh dealt with the Jewish problem. Only when they couldn't protect themselves, let alone compete with Hashem, did they have to withdraw.

It Never Happened Here

Exod. 9:18 says the hail was unprecedented in Egypt. To Ramban, that means there *had* been hail that severe elsewhere; the miracle was geography, not the quantity. Verse 10:14 describes the locusts as unsurpassed in severity, but without limiting it to Egypt. Yet Joel 2:2 warns of locusts that would be more destructive than any that had come before.

Rashi explains that the plague in Joel's time involved several species, whereas Moses' was an unmatched one-species infestation. Ramban disagrees, primarily because the book of Psalms refers to several species decimating the Egyptian crops. He suggests instead that the Torah meant the locusts never had or would descend on Egypt like this, again leaving room for a determined rationalist to categorize the plague as unusual but not unprecedented, and therefore not unnatural.

The modern parallel would be if a prophet predicted a tsunami would hit New York. It might be the first or worst to ever hit New York, but the fact that tsunamis have occurred elsewhere would leave skeptics room to assert that there was nothing supernatural about the event.

It Happened, But Not Naturally

Ramban's second answer offers more reason the Egyptians could fail to see the plague's full import. He suggests the Torah meant there had never been such a swarm of locusts *naturally*, without ruling out supernatural plagues of that level (past or future). An historian of locust swarms might see this one in the upper levels of severity, but not uniquely so, since Hashem might have brought more severe swarms supernaturally—again leaving room to decide that all those swarms, including in Egypt, were natural.

Ramban does think the Jews' immunity to the plagues was an obvious Divine intervention, especially plagues that should have spread. Jews should have suffered from wild animals just like the Egyptians, for example, since no physical boundaries barred the animals from roving into Goshen. He and Sforno add that even in Egypt, the animals ignored Jews they encountered, killing and eating Egyptians instead.

Since the Jews' and Egyptians' grazing lands were next to each other, the pestilence that struck the Egyptian cattle should have continued on to the Jewish cattle, but did not. Even the relatively naturalist Ramban, in other words, saw ample room for the Egyptians to have understood what was actually happening.

Rashi's Miraculous Plagues

On several occasions, Rashi reads the plagues as more miraculous than the text itself requires, making the Egyptians' denial more surprising. For example, when verse 8:2 refers to "the frog" rising from the river (a quirk of Biblical Hebrew, which can refer to many items with a singular noun), Rashi offers the Midrash's literal reading, that only one frog rose; when the Egyptians hit it, it shot out more frogs (we will return to this, when we discuss the Egyptian people's role in the plagues).

At Exod. 9:5, Rashi assumes Moses brought the plague of boils by taking the ashes he and Aaron had gathered in one hand (already a remarkable feat—holding in one hand the content of four fists' worth of ashes), then throwing them up in the air, from where they spread, miraculously, all over Egypt. (Ramban suggests a wind blew them, again providing natural cover for what was happening).

Even still, the Egyptians managed to ignore it all. Can we be confident we would have acted differently? True, they experienced the direct and announced hand of Hashem, but the history of prophecy suggests that wasn't the crucial difference, since our people ignored or rejected the many prophets sent to call us to change.

Watching the plagues go misunderstood, we may need to recognize ourselves, to accept that we all tend to opt for our baseline, to refuse to change even when new information calls for it. Finding ourselves sharing characteristics with the Egyptians should make an urgent goal of changing that aspect of ourselves.

The less obvious Hashem's involvement was and is, the more responsibility it places upon us to see it, to find it. As we work to put ourselves back in the Exodus, a first challenge is to avoid the Egyptians' error of failing to see the supernatural. Tomorrow, we will see that we can often fail to open our eyes. Or we can succeed, as did some of our forefathers back in Egypt.

Natural and Supernatural
in the Rest of the Exodus

We want the supernatural to declare itself, but our commentators see Hashem as hiding His presence sufficiently that even blatant miracles can seem natural. Looking outside the plagues will remind us that part of the greatness of our forefathers was their wisdom in finding the God Who hides. To realize that they, too, could have seen the world as natural reminds us that we see God, even in His most blatant appearances, only if we are open to it.

The Patriarchs Didn't Experience
Hashem Suspending Nature

In Exod. 6:3, Hashem tells Moses He never revealed Himself to the Patriarchs, the *Avot*, with the four-letter Name that we commonly pronounce *Adonai*. Ramban accepts Ibn Ezra's view that that Name signifies Hashem's operating above and outside of Nature. While Hashem saved the *Avot* from famine and other troubles, it happened naturally, such as by telling them to go to places where the famine did not reach.

(This seems to contradict the Talmudic tradition, *Pesachim* 118a, that Abraham survived Nimrod's furnace, a story Ramban himself mentions in his comments on Exod. 20:6. I do not know where or whether he addresses the discrepancy.)

The Exodus will be different, Moses is being told, in that Hashem will make known this Name, meaning that the miracles of the Exodus will tear down the laws of Nature to redeem the Jews. Before that, and many times since, Hashem orchestrates events in ways that can be explained naturally, or as we might say, scientifically. Whole eras, one generation after another, might live in a world that operates with the regularity that fools us into assuming there's no guiding hand or divine intervention. Only when the four-letter Name is being expressed does Hashem break the rules, rather than work within them.

The *Avot*'s leapfrogging the obvious to the fuller picture might be what made them worthy of founding our nation. The Exodus was for the rest of us, who fail to see Hashem in Nature. For us, Hashem provided a one-time Nature-breaking, four-letter-Name-expressing set of events, to sustain us in following our forefathers' path even when that Name does not show itself. Our memories of Egypt and the Exodus aren't about the events alone; they are about Hashem and they remind us to see Him even when it's not easy and obvious.

The Importance and Esotericism of Hashem's Names
The issue of Hashem's Names goes beyond how hard it is to see Hashem's involvement in the world. In Exod. 3:15,

Hashem speaks of the four-letter Name as His Name "לְעֹלָם, *le-olam*, forever." The word is spelled defectively in the Torah, without a *vav*, a combination of letters that can be read as *le-alem*, "to hide."

Rabbinic tradition had it that לעלם hints at the fact that this Name is hidden even in its pronunciation, read differently than written. *Kiddushin* 71a tells of Rava's intending to reveal the true reading of that Name publicly and regularly, despite the prior practice of teaching it to worthy students only once or twice every seven years. He thought it important enough to share with as wide an audience as he could reach. An elder warned him not to, and taught him this verse, with its implication that this Name is not supposed to be public property.

The story shows the balance the Gemara believed in striking between spreading vital information and keeping esoteric that which is too sophisticated for the general public. If we link this to the *Avot* never having seen the four-letter Name, we might say that few of us are vouchsafed an understanding of when and how Hashem breaks through Nature, despite our invoking the Name that refers to it multiple times a day.

For us to come close to reliving those times, we'd have to get better at seeing Hashem's impact when operating within the laws of Nature, and be able to imagine what it would look like when the four-letter Name is functioning. Others around us will insist that no, this too is natural. Will we be able to reject their presumptuous naturalism and recognize Hashem, Who took us out of Egypt?

The Repeat Command to Return to Egypt

After the burning bush, Moses returns to Jethro's house. Tradition explains that he had committed to working for his father-in-law, and felt he needed permission to leave. While there, Hashem appears to him again, at verse 4:19, to tell him to go back to Egypt, and reassures him that all those looking to kill him had died.

Moses apparently needed that reassurance. He was not automatically confident that he would be given supernatural protection, even though Hashem had designated him as the prophet to lead the Jews out of Egypt and as the spokesperson for the upcoming demonstration of Hashem's nature-smashing four-letter Name. Nor does Hashem disagree; He tells Moses that those seeking to kill him have died, not that He, Hashem, would protect Moses from them. In the midst of the most supernatural events in history, Moses correctly has to be aware of when he can and cannot rely on the supernatural.

Room to Misunderstand

When Moses first came to Pharaoh to free the Jews, Pharaoh decided the people had too much time on their hands and ordered his overseers to stop providing building materials. Jewish leaders were punished for the people's failure to meet their quotas, and in turn chastised Moses and Aaron for increasing the nation's suffering. Moses communicated their complaint to Hashem.

Ramban on Exod. 5:22 wonders at this, since Hashem had told him, twice, that Pharaoh would not yield right away.

He reads Moses as having thought that Hashem meant that he would say his piece, Pharaoh would refuse to listen, and the plagues would descend, one after the other, until the Egyptians relented.

The actual plan was for matters to percolate, both before and during the plagues. Ramban thinks, for example, that Pharaoh delayed hearing the Jewish leaders' complaints about the new work rules. Ramban cites the claim from *Shemot Rabbah* 5:19 that Moses returned to Jethro's house for six months before being told to return to initiate the plagues and redemption in earnest.

Part of reliving those times—so we can say "and us He took from there" as sincerely as possible—is to imagine hearing Moses and Aaron's claims of redemption, being convinced by the flashy signs they offered, turning water into blood and a staff into a snake. Then having the crushing disappointment of watching their first foray fall flat, leaving us worse off for several months—including a time when Moses left Egypt, which could easily appear to be an expression of despair.

For how long could ordinary Jews retain faith in Moses, Aaron, and their mission? How long would we?

The First Victory Over the Sorcerers

The second time they come to Pharaoh, Exod. 7:10-12, Aaron and the sorcerers turn their staffs into snakes, but his eats theirs. Rashi fastens on the verse's speaking of the *staff* eating theirs, claiming that this happened after Aaron transformed the snake back into a staff. At this early point, when the sorcerers were sort of keeping up, Rashi thinks there was already enough of a difference for a sensitive observer to realize Moses and Aaron were speaking the greater truth.

Sforno heightens that contrast, arguing that only Hashem animates the inanimate. The sorcerers could make their staffs *look* like snakes, not actually come alive. When Aaron's staff moved on its own, everyone there should have known it was not sorcery.

The Supernatural at the Splitting of the Sea

Commentators' views of the Splitting of the Sea offer one final set of opportunities to add to or detract from how supernatural the events would have looked. In verse 15:2, the Jews say זה א-לי ואנוהו, "this is my God and I will praise Him." Rashi writes that the Jews speak of "this" in celebration of seeing Hashem so clearly as to be able to point a finger. *Kli Yakar* adds that the essence of שירה, *Shirah*, "song," is being able to identify real world events as so clearly the hand of Hashem that we could point, as if an actual hand manifested before us.

Ramban, once again, is more equivocal. He notes that while Moses was told, in Exod. 14:16, to wave his hand over the water to split it, verse 14:21 tells us Hashem brought a strong wind the whole night. Ramban thinks that was deliberate, the veneer of the natural luring the Egyptians to convince themselves it was only the wind.

He reads Exod. 15:18, ה׳ ימלוך לעולם ועד, "Hashem should reign forever," as expressing the hope that in all generations

Hashem will be as clearly revealed as at the Sea. Before we see how he thinks Hashem was so clear, we should pay attention to the fact *that* he thinks it. For all that he read the events of the Exodus as natural-looking, he thought anyone living through those times should have understood Hashem's role in what was happening.

The other way to spot Hashem in the events, for Ramban, was that those who served Him were saved, and those who rebelled were punished, as at the Sea. That's not a useful standard in most generations, where apparently righteous people are oppressed or suffer and apparently evil people succeed, at least temporarily. Yet it was the clarity of justice at the Splitting of the Sea that Ramban saw as the fullest revelation of Hashem we could expect. Full enough that it should have stood as the eternal proof of Hashem's continuing involvement with the world.

Conclusion: Spotting the Supernatural and Learning from It

The complications in spotting even when Hashem's Nature-shattering Name reveals itself seem to me an embodiment of Hosea 14;10's comment, מי חכם ויבן אלה נבון וידעם כי ישרים דרכי יקוק וצדקים ילכו בם ופשעים יכשלו בם, "Who is wise and will understand these, insightful and know them, for the paths of the Lord are smooth, the righteous will go on them and the sinners will stumble on them." The righteous spot and are guided by Hashem where it is not obvious. Sinners ignore the Divine staring them in the face, determined to stay on their road to perdition.

We can test ourselves as to where we would fit along that continuum, one more way to help us put ourselves fully back in those events. How unnatural would an event have to be—one that demanded we change our commitments and values—before we'd admit Hashem was directly involved? Would we do better than the Egyptians? We hope so, but to feel that we left Egypt, we have to move from "hope so" to "pretty sure."

The Human/Divine
Partnership in the Exodus Story

The more we see Hashem hide the supernatural, perhaps to leave room for free will, good and bad, the more we are called to rethink our role in world events. Were there ever to be naked Divine intervention, there would be little room for human input; that Hashem left room even within the Exodus for people to deny its import shows us our first step in doing our part to further Hashem's goals in the world—being open to seeing Hashem's interventions when they appear.

Beyond acknowledging the supernatural, today and tomorrow we will see times when commentators assumed people were supposed to take an active role, and others when they were supposed to be passive. Learning that balance is the next step in figuring out our role in Hashem's world, readying us to relive the Exodus with an eye for how we would want to act were we physically there.

Moses Tells Hashem to Change His Name

Rabbinic literature saw two places in Moses' first prophetic experience where he took an appropriately active role. *Brachot*

9b, quoted in Rashi, pointed out that Hashem originally told Moses that His Name is א-היה אשר א-היה, "I will be what I will be," but closed with the command to say, א-היה, "I will be" sent me to you.

The Gemara attributes the change to Moses' objecting that א-היה אשר א-היה refers to the One Who will be with the Jewish people in all their times of trouble, present and future. While the Jews were still in the throes of a current distress, he said to Hashem, why bring up another one? Hashem accepts his point and adjusts the message.

In that same conversation, at verse 4:10, Moses mentions that he is not a man of words, גם מתמול גם משלשם גם מאז דברך אל עבדך, literally, "also from yesterday, also from the day before, also from when you spoke to your servant." *Shemot Rabbah* 3:14 infers from the uses of "also" that this back and forth stretched a week (yesterday, the day before, from when you first spoke, with each גם adding a day) before Hashem shut it down. Giving Moses that long to argue—and accepting some of his ideas—taught an early lesson, that his input was appreciated, hoped for, even expected.

Hashem Will Only Do It If We Pray For It

Along the same lines, when Moses points to his speech defect as making him unsuitable for the job Hashem has assigned him, Ramban detects a little tug of war. Moses was implying Hashem should have healed him if He wanted him to take the helm of the Jewish people. Hashem, for His part, wanted Moses to pray for it, which Moses didn't want, since that would force him to accept a role he still hoped to avoid.

31

Hashem took another tack, in Ramban's reading, telling Moses his prophecies would contain only words he could say, or that Hashem would ensure the effectiveness of Moses' words even if delivered with his impediment.

Ramban doesn't explain why Hashem insisted on Moses' praying to be healed before He would do it, but it fits the idea that Hashem wants people to take initiative in bringing the future to fruition. It's not an insignificant piece, either; had Moses shown up at court without his speech problems, people who knew him from youth would have been impressed, maybe enough to have the Exodus proceed better than it did. But according to Ramban, that future could only arise if Moses took the first step.

He gives us the opportunity to wonder who contributed to or detracted from the Exodus, what other bright futures did not materialize because in crucial situations people failed to take the first step. Then we can turn that light on ourselves, asking what we would have done had we been there.

Blasphemy and its Punishment:
Better in Person or via Messenger?

In Exod. 5:2, Pharaoh rejects Moses and Aaron's demand to let the Jews go, saying he does not know Hashem and sees no reason to release them. *Sanhedrin* 94a cites R. Yehoshua b. Korchah's assertion that since he blasphemed personally, Hashem took vengeance Himself, as it were; Sennacherib, who left it to his officers to declare that his gods were stronger than Hashem (2 Kings 18), was punished through a messenger.

It's unclear which was better. *Parshat Derachim*, a late 17th-early 18th century work by R. Yehudah Rosanes, understood Pharaoh to have had the courage and interest to take on Hashem himself, as it were, meriting Hashem's "personal" response. He assumed that it's less humiliating to be punished by Hashem than an angel; I add that the Ran suggests (in the fourth of his *Drashot*) that Hashem's direct involvement leaves more flexibility and room for compassion.

The *Torah Temimah, Bereshit* 19, note 13, sees it the other way, that Pharaoh's personal involvement brought the kind of punishment only Hashem administers. He showed the wrong kind of caring and therefore earned an equally more invested, and severe, reaction from Hashem.

Victory Is Easy, Securing Acceptance Is Harder

Exod. 9:10 mentions the boils affecting Egyptian animals, even though verse 9:6 spoke of pestilence killing them all. Rashi explains that the pestilence struck only animals in the fields; some Egyptians heeded Hashem's warning and brought their animals from the fields (as the verse explicitly says happened during hail).

This reminds us that the goal of the plagues was the Egyptians' acquiescence. Victory could have been instant, whenever Hashem decided. As Rashi notes on the words לענת מפני, "to humble yourself before me" (Exod. 10:3), Hashem was trying to help the Egyptians reach submission, recognition, and avowal of Hashem's presence, role, and rule. Those who admitted the plagues were from Hashem, and responded accordingly, were spared the worst, because they helped deepen the Exodus' imprint on world history.

Taking Their Money

In Exod. 11:2, Hashem tells Moses to have the people ask Egyptians for gold and silver, using the word, נא, "please." *Kli Yakar* cites one opinion on *Brachot* 9b, that the Jews did not want the money, fearing it would weigh them down. *Torah Temimah* offers the possibility that the troubles of slavery had doused their appetite for wealth. Whatever the cause, Hashem "needed" them to take it. A tradition of the house of R. Yannai, also on *Brachot* 9b, explains that Hashem was worried about the *Avot* complaining that He had fulfilled the prediction of years of slavery but not the promise of great wealth upon leaving.

The *Torah Temimah* links this to a claim by this same house of R. Yannai, *Brachot* 32a, that Moses defended the Jews after the sin of the Golden Calf by saying that they would not have sinned had Hashem not asked them to take this money. He wonders at the lack of gratitude in misusing money and then blaming that on the donor. For the house of R. Yannai, however, the Jews' resistance to the money, their taking it only at Hashem's request, justified Moses' blaming the sin on Hashem.

How Easily We Get Ourselves in Trouble

Rashi questions why servants' and prisoners' first-born also died, since neither group had the power or freedom to partake of the crimes that incurred this punishment. He answers that the servants enjoyed the Jews' troubles. Delighting in others' evil brought culpability, according to Rashi, even when the ones taking this delight neither benefitted from the evil nor had the power to stop it.

The captive first-born were killed, Rashi says, to prevent the Egyptians' claiming it was their idol that brought the plague. Although Moses announced most of the plagues and those plagues had started and stopped exactly as he said, Rashi followed *Chazal* in thinking the Egyptians would have preferred to assume it was the captive first-born's god(s) who brought the plague, not Hashem.

There are none so blind as those who will not see. Our reliving the Exodus might productively include asking ourselves how far we go to avoid uncomfortable truths. But Rashi's answer raises a moral question as well. Would Hashem kill innocents to avoid others' wrong conclusion about who brought the plagues?

Kli Yakar thinks not, and he insists that the captives deserved what they got, in one of two ways. First, they might have been taken captive only recently, after having had ample time to mistreat Jews. Alternatively, those in jail at night (when the plague struck) mistreated the Jews by day, when they worked outside the jail, as servants. Moses referred to them as servants so Pharaoh could understand why they were being punished, but they were in captivity when the punishment came.

Those out of power might seem free of blame for the wrongs of their society. Rashi sees Hashem weighing degrees of culpability, with even the dispossessed making moral choices. How they handle those moral choices determines what punishments Hashem brings upon them.

People's Role in How Hashem Manifested at the Sea

In the Song of the Sea, Exod. 15:6, the Jews speak twice of Hashem's right hand, when we would have expected the metaphor to refer to a right and a left. Rashi says that when the Jews perform Hashem's Will, the left hand is turned into the right. He does not detail how that works or to what extent, but the comment again gives people some role in deciding how Hashem appears on Earth. We—and, presumably, others who perform Hashem's Will—determine whether the world experiences a right and left hand, or two right ones.

The Song uses the metaphor of God's hands again, in Exod. 15:17, when speaking of His having made a Temple with His hands. Bar Kappara in *Ketubbot* 5a notes that that sets up a contrast with creation, which Isa. 48:13 speaks of as having been done with one hand, whereas מעשה הצדיקים, the actions of the righteous (note that Bar Kappara takes the Temple as an example of actions of the righteous, not an exception to all rules), have both hands helping.

From the greatest prophet to the lowest level of Egyptian society, what we do decides larger and smaller pieces of how the world moves forward. In each instance, we are judged by how well or poorly we contribute to good and help the world combat or move away from evil. That's true in the Exodus and true regarding *mitzvot*, where Hashem defines the right way to use our free will, as we see in the next chapter.

Mitzvot, Shaping the Human
Side of the Partnership with Hashem

While most of the early part of the book of Exodus tells the story of the Jews' leaving Egypt, a few sections shift to promulgating commandments. These first examples of what will become the backbone of the religion, *mitzvot*, show us how Hashem codified our role in hastening the world's redemption and perfection.

Nisan as the First Month

Hashem opens chapter twelve of Exodus with the command to set the calendar by the moon and make Nisan the first month. There are technical *halachic* ramifications to that, such as for counting the years of a king's reign, but Rashi sees it as including an obligation to call the first month "Nisan," the second month "Iyar," and so on.

Ramban assumes the point is to make the Exodus a constant in our lives—every time we mention the date, we will measuring time since the Exodus from Egypt. For him, that explains the *Yerushalmi* saying that we today call the months by names adopted from the Babylonians, fulfilling the predictions of the prophet Jeremiah (16:14), who says on "that day" the Jews will no longer swear by the God Who brought them out of Egypt, but the God Who returned them from the lands of the North (i.e., Babylon).

He tacitly assumes that the mitzvah is to tie the calendar to salvations, not only the Exodus. The Babylonian return was the most recent, and our calendar is one way to keep our awareness of God's salvations present and active.

Intercalation, Active Human Control of the Calendar

The other part of this commandment, the court's right and responsibility to add a month whenever necessary to ensure Pesach happens in spring (some count this as a separate mitzvah), adds to the extent to which Jews are told to see time as a platform for life experience. Jews don't mark time, they define it, corral it into the shape Hashem tells them it needs to follow.

The *Torah Temimah* notes there are limits to which man can exercise control of the calendar. We can add only one month in any year, with no license to alter the months themselves, even for reasons the Talmud saw as valuable, such as to prevent Yom Kippur from falling on a Friday or Sunday.

The first national mitzvah thus includes autonomy, heteronomy, and memory, a common triad within the commandments. We start our years in Nisan, a different month than the rest of the world. We have the right and responsibility to adjust the calendar to make that month happen in the same season as the Exodus it commemorates.

All while accepting limits on our freedom to alter it; we are not masters of the calendar, we are its guardians, with finite but notable rights to guide it as it should go.

To Eat the Sacrifice Is to Experience It

Pesachim 91a tells us that the Pesach sacrifice was necessarily participatory; anyone who couldn't eat a minimum amount (such as someone infirm or ill) could not be listed among those bringing it, even if there were enough others to ensure it was all eaten.

The sacrifice could only be roasted, perhaps to avoid other flavors intruding. On the other hand, it could not be eaten raw or partially cooked, suggesting that its flavor had to be brought out by human effort. The need to foster its taste, but only *its* taste, might explain why it had to be roasted whole, including, as Rashi notes, the intestines, once they had been washed. Only with every piece there would the animal have its full flavor.

Staying in the Houses and the Communities We Join

To explain why the Jews had to stay in their houses when the first-born were being killed, Rashi cites *Bava Kamma* 60a that forces of destruction do not distinguish righteous from wicked once they are unleashed. The *Torah Temimah* generalizes this idea, suggesting we should stay indoors during a plague.

Neither Rashi nor the *Torah Temimah* say this, but the traditional view that tragedies spread beyond their original targets militates in favor of choosing communities carefully.

While forces of destruction can spread across the world, they spread first from their point of origin. If we think of ourselves as reasonably righteous, not deserving plagues but not so great as to merit supernatural divine protection, Rashi and the *Torah Temimah* imply we will be safest if we avoid living among those who deserve punishment, lest their troubles leach over to us.

The Jews lived among the Egyptians against their will, necessitating the blood on the doorposts to differentiate and protect them from what was going on around them. We, who choose where and among whom we build our lives, do not have that supernatural way to immunize ourselves. We have to let our choices of neighbors and neighborhoods do that.

Timing Our Answers and Our Questions

In Exod. 12:26, Moses tells the people of a time when "your children" will ask what this service is. He also supplies the answer, that it is a Paschal sacrifice, commemorating Hashem's having passed over the Jewish houses in Egypt, killing their first-born and saving the Jewish ones.

Despite the Torah's giving no indication of it, the Haggadah made this question famous as that of the *rasha*, the wicked child. The *Kli Yakar* wonders at the Haggadah's giving a different answer than the one in the Torah. His view is that the child's deeming the preparations for Pesach work, asking what it means to the parent, excluding him or herself, makes clear that he or she is on the way out of the religion.

Still, he thinks the Haggadah meant to take that tack only after trying the answer the Torah offered. The first strategy to take with such a child is to strive to draw him or her back with a calm explanation. Only if that fails, the *Kli Yakar* thinks the Haggadah is saying, should we speak harshly.

Aside from his view of how to handle deviation, he reminds us that the same question resonates differently depending on who asks and when, calling for answers appropriate to each circumstance.

Exod. 13:14 speaks of a child who asks, "what's this?" Our *haggadot* call him the תם, the "simple child." Instead of that neutral or charitable term, Rashi calls him a טפש, "stupid or foolish," without enough knowledge to formulate an in-depth question. Barring developmental disabilities, Rashi expects all children to be knowledgeable and engaged enough to pose a detailed question. Anything less is a flaw in the child, and perhaps in those who raised him or her.

That same verse speaks of the child asking מחר, "tomorrow," rather than the usual "in the future." The *Kli Yakar* suggests that it means the day after the sacrifice. Unsure of what was going on, this child understood that asking such a question in the middle of the service would be a challenge; asking afterwards would be a request for information.

How we start a discussion says as much about us as the discussion itself. We can pay close or casual attention, notice details or grasp only the largest part of the picture, issue a challenge or show our interest in being brought into the fold. It starts with us and the attitude we bring.

Tefillin as Expositor of Faith

The Torah speaks of Hashem having taken us out of Egypt "with a strong hand." Ramban, on Exod. 13:16, says the memory of that was supposed to uproot and forestall three kinds of heresy that go back to Enosh. First, that the world is eternal (with inviolable laws of nature, rather than created by Hashem); second, that Hashem has no knowledge of events in this world; and third, that there is no reward and punishment (Hashem *knows* what happens, but does not *react*).

The Exodus was Hashem's one-time refutation of all three, Ramban says, because Hashem is not a performer, rising to each heretic's challenge to prove Himself. By sending a prophet to announce each step of the Exodus, Hashem demonstrated—openly, once and for all—His omnipotence, involvement with the world, and proper remuneration of our actions. It is for the Jewish people to testify to having witnessed these events.

Ramban reminds us that heresies we still see today go far back in human history, and one part of our job is to make clear our belief in the events that refute each of those three claims. In many generations, including ours, heretics point to new proof for their ideas, say that they arrived at their views because of new information, sophistication, or insight, when they are in fact echoing what has been said in other ways before. Part of reliving the Exodus on Seder night is that it reminds us to take up their claims, and to announce our different view of the world and of history.

Making Hashem Beautiful

In the Song of the Sea, Exod. 15:2, the Jews speak of beautifying Hashem (זה א-לי ואנוהו), which *Shabbat* 133b cites as the source for caring about the aesthetics of mitzvah performance, for example, a beautiful *lulav* and a nice *shofar*. Since the verse speaks of glorifying *Hashem*, this reading implies that *how* we perform *mitzvot* adds to that—obeying commandments brings Hashem into the world in one way, but doing it attractively affects how Hashem is perceived in the world, a factor in our choice of how to fulfill the *mitzvot*. *Mitzvot* direct us in how we shape the world, channeling our efforts in some ways and not others. Tomorrow, we'll look a little more at how we can find the limits on our productive contributions to Hashem's plan for history.

The Needle to Thread
in the Human/Divine Partnership

It's important not to exaggerate. For all that we've shown Hashem inviting our creative engagement with His world, for all that we will watch human players succeed or fail in the Exodus, there were other times when Hashem told us exactly how to act, with exact obedience the only legitimate option. Let us pause to see some limits placed on human action, so we can find the middle road of human participation.

The Day We Left Egypt
In Exod. 12:31-33, Pharaoh and his people want the Jews gone immediately. Pharaoh, finally agreeing to what Moses had been asking, with no conditions or limitations, ran to find Moses in the middle of the night, to chase him out of Egypt.

It still wasn't the right move. Ramban quotes a *Mechilta* that sees Moses as telling Pharaoh that the Jews wouldn't steal away in the night like thieves. Leaving wasn't good enough; they had to leave in broad daylight, where everyone could see that the Egyptians had acquiesced to Hashem's demands.

A similar idea is echoed in an interpretation of בעצם היום הזה, "in the middle of this day" (Exod. 12:41). The Midrash (*Sifrei Devarim* 337) understands that phrase as contravening the people who sought to foil the divine plan. To prove that Hashem's plan would not be compromised, Hashem made the Exodus happen in broad daylight, not in the cover of darkness, which would have spared Pharaoh further embarrassment. That Midrash relates a similar incident about the generation of the flood, which swore they would never let Noah enter the ark (Gen. 7:13, which uses the same Hebrew phrase). (The *Midrash Tannaim*, Deut. 32:48, adds a final case—that of Abraham's circumcision.)

The Midrash sees Pharaoh clinging to any power, even if only to order the Jews to leave immediately, to help hide the futility of himself and his people. It should remind us of the error in the human urge for—even obsession with—control. It is a natural human desire to assert some sense of being in charge. After all the plagues, after being forced to do that which he repeatedly refused, Pharaoh still tries to dictate when and how the Jews go. Watching him reminds us to avoid imitating him. When we relive the Exodus this year, we should be enlightened enough to realize that we cannot assert control in every situation and sometimes we're supposed to do as we're told.

The Sensitivity of Hashem's System

Commentators saw Moses' choices as also more limited than we might have thought. In Exod. 4:21, Hashem reminds him of the wonders he is supposed to perform before Pharaoh.

Ramban reads that as a call to review them: to be sure he remembered to turn the water into blood, show his hand affected by *tsaraat* and then healed, and turn the staff into a snake, as well as an admonishment to pay careful attention to the wonders to come, to perform them exactly as told. Ramban cites a Midrash (*Shemot Rabbah* 5:6) that the acronym for the plagues we mention during the Seder in the name of R. Yehudah, דצ״ך, עד״ש, באח״ב, was engraved on the staff.

Ramban does not explain the need for reminders, especially since Hashem tells Moses what to do again before each plague. Why admonish him to review, give him a staff with hints to the names of the plagues, when He was going to repeat it again in its proper time?

Sforno suggests it reflects the exactness needed, a warning that any change from his directions might impair the process. Moses had no guarantee the wonders would happen unless he followed the necessary procedure. If he performed it incorrectly, and miracles didn't occur, it would look as if Hashem hadn't sent him.

However, we don't see this level of specifity in the text itself. Even though Moses was to lead the Exodus, Ramban and Sforno are concerned that he would not properly follow directions, and these commentators further worry that even a small deviation could influence the result. Moses, the greatest of prophets, the greatest servant of God, reaches his stature by accepting what God tells him, not by instituting a plan of his own.

Sforno extends this to *mitzvot* in general, saying that to change any detail of an observance might compromise the mitzvah-act of its power and meaning. Moses' need to obey God's instruction emphasizes the specificity of the commandments. So while it is true that free will, choice, and action matter, they operate in a narrower band than we might realize.

Hashem's Being Noticed in the Song and in the World

To use our freedom in ways that contribute, we have to understand Hashem's plan for the world. However, as the Sforno shows in a series of comments, this might not be intuitive. In Exod. 15:2, the Jews sing of Hashem as their God and the God of their forefathers. They experienced a God Who drowned the Egyptians in the Sea, but they were also clear that this was the same God that their forefathers announced to the world, such as when Jacob built an altar to celebrate Hashem's mercy and justice (Gen. 33:20).

That's also the message of the next verse, when the Jews speak of Hashem as a "man of war," adding that His "Name" is Hashem. For Sforno, they mean that the name Hashem is appropriate even for the איש מלחמה, the "man of war," that these distinct and even contradictory effects on the world extend from the same, unified Hashem. That's because the destruction of evildoers is an act of both justice and mercy.

Weeding a garden punishes the weeds, but is an act of kindness in that it provides space for the rest of the garden to grow. Today we often recoil from any type of death, but Sforno says that the death of some evildoers is good for everyone else. (He also cites a tradition that the wind that split the Sea froze it so the Jews could pass on dry land; it then moved to cover the Egyptians, stopping them from escaping, another act of mercy coupled with an act of justice).

Sometimes we are to do nothing and must let Hashem run events. Sometimes we are to do exactly as we are told. Here, we see that when we have free will, when we are called to partner with Hashem, we need to allow the "characteristics" of Hashem to teach us how to use our own free will. When we see that the Jews understood that Hashem melds the duality of justice and mercy into a unified whole, we understand our own limitations and how much more work there is still left for us to do.

Room to Fail

The Talmud gives a unique interpretation of the verse מי כמכה באלים ה', "who among the gods is like You, O Lord" (Exod. 15:11). The Talmud (*Gittin* 56b) reads the word אלים, which normally means "gods" or "powerful ones" as אלמים, "silent ones." Hashem stays silent, as it were, and keeps His Presence in the background so as to give humans room to err and to make choices without being directly aware of Hashem's Providence. This is the greatest show of His power.

Free will must include the possibility of its abuse. Based on the verse which uses the phrase עד יעבר, "until it [i.e., Israel] will come" (Exod. 15:16), the Talmud says that Hashem's plan was to have the second entrance to Israel (in

49

Ezra's time) be as miraculous as when the Jews entered in Joshua's time. However, because of the Jews' sins, the second entrance was not as spectacular.

The sense of lost opportunities, the Talmud tells us, is embedded even in our moments of greatest praise— wonderful as it was, it could have been more so had we acted better. Part of reliving the Exodus, I suggest, is putting both sides of that coin at the forefront of our consciousnesses: the potential granted us with free will, the places where we are allowed or supposed to act on that free will (and its limitations), along with the possibility of failure.

To make that standard more concrete, let's turn our attention to how the most prominent actors in the Exodus used their free will. Did Pharaoh, the Egyptians, the Jews, and Moses succeed, fail, neither, or both? Reading how they performed, and thinking to ourselves what we would have done, serves the dual purpose of reminding us of the story, so we can tell it better, and of bringing it to life in ways that affect us personally, helping to transform the recitation into reliving, which is our central goal.

Moses' Successes in Egypt

Figuring out how to balance submission to Hashem with making creative contributions to His plan for the world, deciding when each is appropriate, is a general life task. It also offers a convenient rubric for evaluating the major players in the Exodus. Watching Moses, the Jewish people, the Egyptians, and Pharaoh succeed or fail will take us deeper into the story, move us along the path to feeling as if we ourselves had been there, and then left.

I start with Moses because he was the most clearly successful of the four (one could easily argue that Aaron was more successful, but the text and commentators say too little about him to justify a whole discussion; suffice it to say that he acquitted himself quite well at least until the sin of the Golden Calf). Cataloging the successes commentators found in Moses' actions, and then (in tomorrow's entry) his failures, we will be reminded of the complications of judicious use of free will.

Moses Is Born Great

In Exod. 1:16, Rashi takes the view that Pharaoh decided to drown the Jewish males because his astrologers told him a redeemer was about to be born. At his birth, Moses' mother sees כי טוב הוא, that he is "good" (Exod. 2:2), which Rashi reads according to the Talmud that the house filled with light. Not only was he "good," but it was clear to everyone that he was destined for greatness. Five verses later, Rashi thinks Moses refused to nurse from Egyptian women because such as act was unseemly for someone who would speak with Hashem.

For Rashi, Moses was destined to be the redeemer, filled the house with light at his birth and, as a newborn, instinctively rejected milk that would sully him. That may be purely historical rather than intended to make a point, but either possibility makes Moses almost superhuman from his earliest moments, leaving us little to learn; that which we cannot hope to imitate is also not a model towards which to strive.

The Moses We Can Try to Be

Other commentators portray a more relatable Moses. The *Torah Temimah* cites opinions that Moses' original name was טוב, "goodness," or טובי-ה, "the goodness of Hashem." The *Torah Temimah* also quotes the opinion that Moses was born circumcised, his exceptional qualities being expressed as bodily realities. This still assumes that, at birth, his potential was clear to all, but not in the miraculous way that Rashi presented.

Ramban picks up on the superfluity of saying Jochebed saw Moses was good; most or all mothers see goodness in their children! For him, it means she saw something (perhaps

Rashi's light) to lead her to believe the baby would *survive*. Other mothers loved their babies as much as Jochebed loves her son, and they also must have made efforts to save them. But, convinced that all hope was lost, they made only futile gestures. According to Ramban, when the text refers to Moses as "good," it means his mother saw a reason that he would survive. (If she told him this as she nursed him, it would instill a sense of personal destiny.)

Moses was not like us; he was born with some of his future greatness already embedded. Reading his story won't be a matter of seeing if we would have done as he did. Rather, it will be a matter of seeing to what extent he fulfilled his own potential. It is a reminder that success isn't guaranteed, even for Moses, and that Hashem's call challenges each of us to stretch beyond what's easy for each individual, even for Moses.

Moses Achieves Greatness

Moses' growing up is mentioned twice, in Exod. 2:10-11, which is a seeming redundancy. Rashi explains that the first mention indicates his maturation, and the second refers to his rise in the court, since (according to Rashi) Pharaoh named him head of his household. The verses together tell us he grew up and, from that early age, demonstrated leadership capabilities.

Ramban reads those verses as referring first to weaning and then to adulthood. Moses only becomes a leader when he decides to investigate the Jews' condition. Once he was told that he was a Jew, that knowledge created a strong enough connection for him to want to see their condition.

That same connection, or the sense of justice Ramban sees in other events in Moses' life, moved Moses to kill the Egyptian who was beating a Jew. Ramban sees Moses, who was raised as Pharaoh's daughter's son, climbing the ladder of Egyptian leadership, yet also inculcated with (or choosing to feel) a bond with his brethren strong enough to risk and lose his position in Pharaoh's palace.

This was a choice of path and identity that wasn't obvious or unavoidable; it was a choice Moses made. For all the gifts Moses was born with, Ramban sees him taking real risks, without any assurance Hashem would protect him from the consequences.

Here, we can wonder whether we would have been like Moses, because his choice was not superhuman or gifted him from birth. What risks would we take on behalf of others with whom we have a tenuous connection? Would the injustice of one man beating another—especially where our more immediate cultural bond is with the perpetrator— lead us to risk all we have to save the victim?

Moses' Unquenchable Sense of Justice

In the short term, it cost him. He was exposed, Pharaoh sentenced him to death, and he fled. Ramban dates those events to his youth, and his marriage to Zipporah to years later, just before he was sent back to Egypt to start the redemption (since his second child, Eliezer, seems to have been a newborn).

Despite that blank space in his biography, his saving Jethro's daughters from the other shepherds shows he had not lost his insistence on justice. Ramban points out that it's particularly remarkable for a fugitive; Moses spent half a century or more fleeing Pharaoh, and he was worried enough about what awaited in Egypt that when he was sent back, Hashem had to assure him that those searching for him had died.

But when Jethro's daughters were being mistreated, Moses didn't think twice. As with the Egyptian he killed, his rage at the shepherds' taking water they had not drawn overwhelmed his humility. For Ramban, had the other shepherds only forced the daughters to wait until they were done, he might not have intervened; but the girls had come early and filled the troughs. By banishing them, the shepherds were stealing the fruit of the women's labors, and Moses would not ignore such an injustice. The avoidance of petty theft, not the need to remake the world, moved Moses to action.

Reaching the Burning Bush:
Moral Fiber or Meditation and Seclusion
Moses' concern with avoiding theft underlies Rashi's reading of the phrase אחר המדבר (Exod. 3:1), which is used to describe how Moses tended his sheep. For Rashi, that expresses Moses' יראת חטא, being so concerned to avoid the sin of petty theft that he tended his sheep deep in the desert.

Sforno suggests his location also allowed him to be מתבודד ומתפלל, to go into meditative seclusion and pray. These are the actions of aspiring prophets. Sforno portrays

Moses as gravitating to the lifestyle of a prophet, whether or not he actively sought prophecy.

Do we avoid acting wrongly, shape our surroundings to remove the possibility—not just the actuality—of wrongdoing? Alternatively, do we choose a lifestyle that leads us in a positive direction, whether or not we have a particular outcome in mind? For Rashi and Sforno, Moses did both, in ways that the rest of us could do as well, if we so chose.

Bones and Booty

The Torah goes out of its way to note that Moses took Joseph's bones with him when the Jews left Egypt. This fulfilled the oath Joseph administered to his brothers, saying that when they left Egypt, they should take his bones with them. This might count as a failure of the people, too caught up in preparing for the Exodus to fulfill their long-standing obligation, but we can consider it here, in the more positive context of it showing that Moses held a firm focus on what matters most.

The *Kli Yakar* thinks Moses deliberately sought a mitzvah that expressed different values from the rest of the people. Everybody else was rushing around for gold and silver, but Moses was focused on *mitzvot*, choosing the mitzvah of honoring the wishes of the dead because it stressed the ephemerality of physical possessions while the other Jews were caught up in securing them. *Sotah* 9b sees this as why Hashem Himself later buried Moses, as it were; since Moses involved himself with Joseph's burial, Hashem repaid the favor.

Sforno takes the opposite view. He claims it was Moses' responsibility, since he was the leader and representative of the people from whom Joseph had extracted the oath. According to Sforno, Moses did his job, nothing more.

A quick turn through Moses' actions shows us a man born great, raised to be great, and developing himself towards that greatness. Whatever advantages he started with, commentators highlight his sense of responsibility and justice, his acting in ways that seemed important and vital, whatever the cost to himself.

Once he encounters Hashem, Moses struggles to inhabit his role through much of the rest of the Exodus. Later in the Torah we again see him succeeding a great deal, but until the Splitting of the Sea, we see many examples of his not doing as well as he might. As we'll see tomorrow.

The Failures of Moses

Pointing out others' failures can be smug one-upsmanship or, as I hope it will be for us, it can be a reminder that it's never easy, for any of us. Especially since we've just seen the greatness Moses had at birth and then developed, seeing that even he did not always manage to take his best next step helps us in two ways. It alerts us to the need to be on the lookout for failure—since even Moses went there—but also reminds us to never let those failures fool us into thinking we cannot still accomplish great deeds.

We look at Moses because it's easier than looking at ourselves. If we open our minds enough, it can spark our thoughts about what we would have done and let us plan for a better future, use his experience to improve our chances of fulfilling our potential.

Moses' Concern for His Brother

The first time Moses acts less than perfectly is when Hashem tells him he has been chosen as the prophet to lead the Jews out of Egypt. Moses resists, at length—an example, as we saw previously, of his taking advantage of his Hashem-invited opportunity to debate the Divine plan and successfully offer adjustments to it.

His last words before Hashem shuts down the conversation are שלח נא ביד תשלח, "send please through the hands of whom You will send" (Exod. 4:13). Rashi thinks that refers to Aaron, then the leader of the slaves in Egypt and their prophet. Moses worried that his surpassing him would insult his brother. Why would Hashem turn to a new messenger when there was already one in place?

The Torah tells us this was the wrong move; before we look at that, let us note the family drama in this moment. It was daunting enough that he was being told to publicly lead the Exodus, and to take on the leadership of a people he hadn't seen in decades. Moses was also going to supplant his older brother, who had stayed in Egypt all these years. While Moses had been out of the picture, Aaron had worked with the people, suffered with them, served as their prophet, and strove to keep them as close to Hashem as possible. Moses was being told to swoop in and supersede him.

His resistance crossed a line, as we're about to see, but as we review the sources that portray him as being in the wrong, let's remember some of the pressures that might have pushed him to act as he did.

Failure and Consequences

Exod. 4:14 describes Hashem as reacting with חרון אף, "wrath," although we are not told how or why he should have known it was time to stop. R. Yehoshua b. Korchah, at

Zevachim 102a, says the Torah only uses that phrase when it comes with a punishment, and he wonders why we do not see one here. R. Shimon b. Yochai replies that there was a punishment, because Aaron was given the High Priesthood, not Moses. In his view, Hashem's original plan was that Moses would be High Priest as well as prophet and political leader, while Aaron would be an ordinary Levite.

Today, we recoil from such centralized power; perhaps Moses' mishandling of his job justifies these concerns, perhaps it's the reason Hashem's חרון אף took this form. But we have to notice that R. Shimon b. Yochai thought Hashem originally believed there was value in Moses filling all those roles. Perhaps only someone as exceptional as Moses outweighed the problems of centralization of power, but in that instance, it seems to have been the preferred course.

Exacerbating the sting of never knowing how the world would have looked had Moses not crossed this line, his protest turned out to be pointless. Hashem tells him that Aaron would rejoice fully when he saw his brother in his new role. For Ramban, Hashem was saying that Aaron was so selfless that he would have come of his own volition to help Moses once he heard of his brother's mission. Aaron was not only unconcerned with his own honor, but he was also eager to contribute however he could.

His failure to recognize his brother's humility lost Moses the High Priesthood. The rest of us may never know what we lost.

Moses and Zipporah at the Inn

Exod. 4:24-26 tells the story of an angel threatening either Moses or his son at the inn. The Talmud (*Nedarim* 31b) assumes the angel came because Moses failed to circumcise his son at his first practical opportunity. For someone like Moses, a lack of alacrity could have been considered a capital crime (unless we assume the angel was there only to *threaten* death) despite his having just been appointed the central figure of the Exodus.

This event is a reminder that we sometimes excuse our own failings too quickly. Moses does something that may seem truly minimal—delaying a circumcision—yet *Chazal* saw it as a serious failure. They also assumed the plasticity of Hashem's plans. Hashem chose Moses, we would think, because he was the best messenger. A subtext of the story is that had he died at the inn, Hashem's plan for history (and the redemption of the Jews) would have had to occur another way.

The question is never whether the will of Hashem is going to be done; it is how much of our slated role each of us will contribute. This time, in Rashi's reading, Zipporah saves the day, avoiding the consequences of Moses' failure, and letting him live to fulfill more of his destiny.

Moses' Doubt as a Reason Not to Enter the Land

At the end of chapter 5 (after the officers of the people accosted him for worsening their situation), Moses complains to Hashem that the redemption has not yet happened. Hashem says, עתה תראה, "now you will see what I will do to Pharaoh"

(Exod. 6:1). Rashi writes that because of his doubts, Moses would see *now*, and only what would be done to Pharaoh. He would not see what would be done in the future to the Canaanite kings.

Rashi later says several times that Moses only lost his right to enter Israel when he hit the rock at Meribah (e.g., on Num. 20:12). However, the discussion in *Sanhedrin* 111a, quoted by Rashi, times Moses' loss of the right of entry to Israel to this moment. It also contrasts Moses' conduct to that of the patriarchs, who never complained, despite seeing few of Hashem's promises fulfilled.

We have no reason to think we'd have done better, but it's still an example of where the story went in a different direction from the ideal. The Jews *could* have had Moses march them to the Land instead of Joshua, with all the ripples for future history that would have brought, if only Moses had not complained here (and not hit the rock later).

The Problem with Moses' Call to Hashem

In Exod. 14:15, as the Jews are huddled at the Sea, watching the Egyptians bear down, Hashem asks Moses why he's crying to Him. Rashi reads that as a rebuke for praying during a time for action, another instance where Moses seems to have been expected to know what to do even without direct orders. However that was supposed to happen, it didn't here; Moses didn't realize he was supposed to lead, not pray.

Ramban lets Moses off easier, seeing the rebuke as about the urgency with which he called Hashem, being צועק,

"screaming," rather than asking. Moses (and the Jewish people) need to learn, according to Ramban, that faith leads to a prayerful but confident approach, not flailing or screaming, even when matters seem desperate. Ramban sees Moses as being told to ask, "How should we do this, Hashem?" rather than crying, "Oh, no, please save us, Hashem!"

Sforno once again takes the verse in a wholly different direction. He understands that Moses was complaining that the Jews would never trust him enough to enter the water on his orders alone. When Hashem says מה תצעק אלי, "why are you calling to Me," Sforno reads that as a rebuke for thinking ill of the people, who in fact would listen to him.

Born with the greatness that made him the one to lead the Jews out of Egypt, Moses' first months in that role were, by one standard, wildly successful. He was the faithful servant who performed the tasks Hashem told him, bringing the Jews out of Egypt, through the Red Sea, and permanently away from their former masters. The readings we just reviewed show that the commentators saw other elements to his tenure, that often even apparently tremendous achievements could have been that much better.

But perhaps Moses was too great to serve as a model. Tomorrow, we'll look at how our commentators view the Jewish people's handling of the Exodus. Perhaps this will be a closer enough parallel, which can help us turn our thoughts towards what we would have done.

Seeds That Could Have
Led to Success for the Jewish People

The Jewish people are us; as we watch our ancestors succeed (today's chapter) and fail (tomorrow's), we should remember that this is who we were back then. Is it who we would be if the same events (or parallel events) happened today?

The Tribes, Hashem's Love
for Them, and Their Traditions

The book of Exodus starts by naming the sons of Jacob who came to Egypt. Rashi cites *Chazal's* statement that this and other enumerations of the tribes are a sign of Hashem's love, comparable to Isaiah's statement about the stars, "Who takes their hosts out by number, to each by name He calls" (Isa. 40:26).

In their original context, Isaiah's words caution us against seeing creation as impersonal. Naming each star shows that Hashem deals with each on its own terms, responding to each one's individual characteristics. Creation is not a giant process set in motion and then ignored; Hashem keeps track of the large and small pictures.

When Rashi relates that to the enumeration of the tribes, it tells us that each of Jacob's sons was also valued individually, and their character shaped that of the tribe that descended from them. Like the stars who are cherished for their individuality, the tribes play specific and necessary roles as Hashem's people, and are therefore enumerated wherever possible.

That rationale also implies that each unit of the people held onto its ancestor's character. The slavery in the book of Exodus happens to a people whose citizens bear allegiance to the larger nation as well as to their tribal subgrouping. They kept alive tribal traditions, separate from those of the nation, as well as traditions of the nation as a whole. And they will leave in tribes, a permanent aspect of their national personality.

Names, Language, and
Belief in the Coming Redemption
Rabbinic literature held that the traditions they kept alive were names, language, and dress. The *Kli Yakar* thinks each of the brothers' names alluded to the redemption; retaining their names kept alive their hopes for leaving Egypt. *Reuven*, for example, includes the verb for "to see," a reminder that Hashem would eventually "see" their troubles.

The *Kli Yakar*'s logic explains the necessity of knowing Hebrew. Reuben is just a name, *Reuven* has a message for someone who speaks Hebrew. The Midrash celebrates the Jews' holding on to their language because it meant they would understand the names, and they would remember the upcoming redemption.

A Separate Sexual Morality
and an Avoidance of Slander

The *Kli Yakar's* version of that Midrash had sexual morality, not dress, as the third component (perhaps "dress" in our version hints at sexual morality, not simply a way to look different). When the first verse of the book refers to the tribes' coming with Jacob to the land of Israel, the *Kli Yakar* sees it as a hint that they held to the Patriarch's value system, particularly his resistance to sexual immorality.

For him, that's also why the verse stresses that each of Jacob's sons was married when he arrived in Egypt. Otherwise, some of the sons might have married Egyptian women and would have absorbed some of their perverted worldview. (The Egyptians, in Rabbinic tradition, were שטופי זימה, saturated in sexual immorality, along with their various forms of idolatry.)

The *Kli Yakar's* version of the Midrash said the Jews also retained their rejection of slander, which is why they knew where the Egyptians kept their gold and silver—the Egyptians knew they could trust their discretion, so they told them (note that he equates avoiding slander with maintaining confidences).

Before the Exodus, the Jews had a national character, an awareness of each tribe's role within that nation, a connection to their past, and a firm hope for their future. And that trustworthiness would make them rich.

What Helped the Jews Accept Moses as the Redeemer

Hashem tells Moses to use the words פקד פקדתי, that Hashem has taken note of what is happening to them (Exod. 3:16). Rashi suggests the Jews had a tradition that their savior would use these words, since Jacob and Joseph had said them before their passing (the text has Joseph saying it twice, in Gen. 50:24-5; Rashi assumes the first presents what Jacob had said, the second is his speaking on his own behalf).

In this view, Jacob and Joseph had used those words specifically to establish the code for how to recognize their redeemer. And the Jews had retained that memory.

Moses assumed the Jews would not believe him, for which Hashem punished him with *tsara'at* (Exod. 4:6-7). This fed into another tradition, which said that anyone who tried to hurt them (including by slander) would be afflicted with bodily plagues (such as when Pharaoh and Abimelech were stricken for taking Sarah from Abraham).

For all that Rashi accepts the Midrashic view that the Jews retained only their names, language, and dress, these comments show only one aspect of their national identity. Their memories of the words that Jacob and Joseph used, and of how Hashem protected Abraham and Sarah, were an additional part of their continuing national memory.

The question of retained traditions reverberates through Jewish history, especially at our Passover Seder, when Jews of all levels of knowledge come together. As we reinsert ourselves in that story, what does or doesn't last is surely a part of the puzzle.

The Genealogy of Moses

One tribe seems to have remembered more than the others, giving it a privileged position in the future nation. We see this in Ramban's reading of chapter six. Starting at verse 6:14, the Torah rehearses the genealogy of Reuben, Shimon, and Levi, culminating with Moses and Aaron. Rashi says the goal was always to get to Moses and Aaron; the inclusion of Reuben and Shimon was only to start from Jacob's eldest.

Ramban says they are there as contrast to show that Moses, Aaron, and their tribe earned the positions they were about to be given, not inherited them. The Torah told us the first generation of those tribes, hinting that they were the ones worthy of mention; their descendants quickly joined Egyptian culture. Ramban describes Levi's descendants, down to Moses' time, as חסידי עליון, "righteous servants of the Most High."

Sforno attributes the greater success of Levi's tribe to his long life, because he was still around to help raise his children and grandchildren in the paths of Hashem.

Between them, Ramban and Sforno remind us of the fragility of righteousness and the difficulty of transmitting it to generations to come. We can all hope to reproduce Levi's success, whether by being granted his personal longevity or some other reason. When we relive the story, we can all decide to strive to imitate that aspect of Levi's legacy.

A Mark of Leadership

Exod. 5:10-21 pauses to tell us of the officers of the Jewish people, who were held accountable for meeting the daily quotas. According to Rashi, the Egyptians, like many oppressors, set up a bureaucracy in which Jews managed Jews. It was the Jewish leaders who had to tell their brethren that Pharaoh would no longer provide building materials but still expected the building to proceed at the same pace as before.

In later history, some Jews took on such roles for personal and familial benefit, and to secure special privileges from the oppressor. The officers in Egypt did the opposite; they used their position to *shield* the people. When production slipped, now that they had to find materials as well as build, the Egyptians beat the שוטרים, the Jewish officers, expecting them to pass it along, communicating the necessity of building more and faster.

They didn't. Not only that, but Exod. 5:19 notes that they saw their brothers' troubles ברע, "badly," which Rashi reads as meaning that they sympathized with them. While they themselves were being beaten, they retained their ability to feel how difficult life had become for their fellow Jews. Their reward, Rashi says, was that they became the Sanhedrin, meriting a visitation of the Divine Presence that rested on Moses.

They set a high standard for Jewish leadership. A prime characteristic of members of the Sanhedrin and those who merit visitation by the Divine is the willingness to bear the personal costs of staring down injustice, retaining compassion for those whom evildoers try to turn into their "cause."

In Exod. 12:35-36, the Jews follow Moses' command and ask the Egyptians for gold and silver. Ramban thinks that's more than avarice—it indicates an admission that they had been wrong to blame Moses for the slow start to the process.

Ramban turns a casual verse about money into a crucial moment of the redemption, when people came to sign on to the truths Moses had been espousing for months, and recognized they should have done so earlier. This leaves us to wonder when we would admit that our rejection of some idea had been wrong and concede that a call for us to change our behavior or worldview was in fact exactly on point.

The Jews were not unequivocally successful during the Exodus, as we'll see tomorrow. But without ignoring or minimizing their failures, we should remember the strengths they brought, their retained awareness of their past, their seeing themselves as links in a chain, their having held on to key components of that chain—names, language, dress (and/or sexual morality), awareness of the coming redemption and the words the redeemer would say, and of Hashem's punishing those who aim to harm them.

Some groups did even better. The Levites stayed true to their heritage as servants of God (and avoided slavery, as we'll see tomorrow); the officers of the people held fast to their sense of connection with their fellow Jews, even at personal cost.

These are the positives our people brought to the Exodus story. As we relive the tale, we should be sure to do no worse. Or even to do better.

Dragging Down the Redemption

The distance of history reassures us that listing the failures of the generation that left Egypt will not seem like we are judging them or pretending any confidence we would have done better. We enumerate where they went wrong to teach ourselves how to avoid repeating the past, to make our reliving of the Exodus an act of constructive and productive memory, not a rote rehearsal of a list of events.

Done right, we can walk away better than we walked in, readier to react optimally when it is our turn to be tested. A full awareness of the stumbles of our predecessors can help us avoid those failures going forward.

Bringing Slavery upon Ourselves

In Exod. 1:10, Pharaoh justifies enslaving the Jews with the claim that they would join the Egyptians' enemies in case of war, ועלה מן הארץ, most easily read as "and leave the land." But if they were potential enemies, commentators have long noted, he should *want* them to leave!

Sforno makes the fascinating but radical suggestion that Pharaoh *did* want the Jews gone, that this phrase was part of his *plan*, not a fear. Since the Jews are so dangerous, he said, let us act wickedly towards them, and they will leave. His goal was to be rid of them, not enslave them (Sforno would have to say that Pharaoh changed his mind later, perhaps because the Egyptians got used to the luxuries of having slaves).

For Sforno, the Jews of that first generation were unwittingly complicit in their sufferings, their excessive focus on staying in Egypt blinding them to Pharaoh's message. The subsequent history of Egyptian mistreatment was, in this reading, partially a result of the Jews' own failure to leave when given the opportunity. That does not pardon the Egyptians' crimes, but it shows a Jewish failure to take freedom when offered.

The *Torah Temimah* has another way the Jews contributed to their own enslavement. He cites R. Eliezer in *Sotah* 11b, that the slavery is described as עבודת פרך, "backbreaking labor," to hint at פה רך, "soft mouth." Pharaoh fooled the Jews with soft words, step by step until they were slaves.

R. Eliezer does not elaborate. The *Torah Temimah* assumes Pharaoh announced a public works project, which he joined the first day. The Jews were eager to prove their civic pride. Thinking it a one-day job, they gave extraordinary effort. Pharaoh then made that day's output their daily quota going forward.

Sforno thinks the Jews' attachment to Egypt got them in trouble, while the *Torah Temimah* thinks it was their concern with proving their dedication to their adopted country. They agree that the Jews were part of the reason the slavery was what it was. It started with descendants of Jacob forgetting he had told them to feel like strangers in this land, waiting for when Hashem returned them to the land promised to their forefathers.

Jewish Sins that Contributed to Slavery

On Moses' second excursion to check the welfare of his brethren, he sees two Jews fighting, and upbraids one for intending to hit the other (Exod. 2:13). The fighters (whom tradition identifies as Dothan and Abiram) react badly. The assailant challenges Moses' right to mix in, mockingly asking whether he intends to kill him, as he had the Egyptian.

The verse comments that Moses became afraid, realizing "the matter was known." Rashi notes a Midrash that he had wondered, until then, what made the people deserve this slavery. With these words, he understood that they were talebearers.

The comment assumes slavery was a punishment, not only preparation for nationhood. Further, it considers talebearing a serious enough transgression to justify slavery, a traditional perspective we might forget to keep in mind.

The *Kli Yakar* echoes that when explaining why Hashem chose to appear to Moses in the image of a burning bush. We've seen before that the *Kli Yakar* had a different tradition of what the Jews held on to—while we often say it was their clothes, names, and language, he had it as their sexual morality, names, and language. His version added another element as well, that they held on to their ancestral abjuring of slander and gossip. Dothan and Abiram's threat to reveal that Moses killed the Egyptian showed that they had abandoned this practice.

But, the *Kli Yakar* adds, their refusal to slander others was only in their dealings with outsiders. The burning bush made the point that even as they were being consumed with suffering (burning), the Jews were still sticking their thorns into each other, another reason they had not yet merited redemption.

Beyond the question of slander, the *Kli Yakar* thinks their overall assimilation meant they needed a process before they could even leave. That's why Exod. 3:10 speaks of taking them out of Egypt, not the *land* of Egypt. They first had to separate from its society and culture, and only after that would they be ready to exit the physical location.

Not Ready for Redemption, Even When the Time Had Come

When Exod. 2:25 speaks of Hashem's "seeing" the Jews' sufferings and knowing it was time, the *Torah Temimah* quotes *Yerushalmi Ta'anit* that includes the Jews' repentance as part of what earned them the right to leave. Ramban, Sforno, and the *Kli Yakar* all ignore that, seeing the Jews as not yet deserving redemption.

Ramban says that the multiple verbs describing Hashem's decision to save the Jews—heard, remembered the covenant, saw, and knew—stress that the Jews were redeemed only because of their cries for mercy. Strict justice would have left them to languish, a view Ramban repeats on Exod. 12:40 to explain why the verse says the Jews were in Egypt for 430 years instead of the 400 predicted to Abraham. While Rashi counts the extra years to an earlier start date, Ramban says the Jews in fact left later than originally promised, because they did not deserve to leave.

Sforno thinks only the oppressors' cruelty tipped the scales for redemption (on Exod. 2:23).

The *Kli Yakar* reflects on that verse's speaking separately of their plaints from the work and then their crying to Hashem, and offers two explanations. He first posits that their cries were internal, sadness at what was happening to them. The next verb, ויזעקו, "they cried out," was their call for redemption, which they felt certain they deserved.

The verse disagrees, *Kli Yakar* says, attributing Hashem's decision to redeem them to their cries מן העבודה, "from the work," not the זעקה, the crying out. This is a double failure (and, sadly, a common one), not managing to deserve the good Hashem waits to give us, and not reading ourselves honestly, making it harder to improve.

The *Kli Yakar*'s second suggestion is that there were two types of Jews. Good ones cried out for help with no sense they deserved it. Others grumbled *at* Hashem, certain this was Divine injustice. The verse telling us that Hashem listened to the cries from the work tells us which group had it right; the same idea as in his first suggestion, namely that some or many Jews had a false picture of themselves and of Hashem.

The *Kli Yakar* gives more than a hint that his ideas are fueled by events in his own time, insights into his contemporaries that he assumes would have characterized the Jews of the Exodus. They ring true for us as well.

Not Believing in Moses or His Promises

We see some of the Jews' difficulties with faith, where the verse explains that the people did not heed Moses מקוצר רוח ומעבודה קשה, "from shortness of breath (or spirit) and hard labor" (Exod. 6:9). Rashi takes it literally, that people in distress cannot breathe deeply; their inability to hear was almost physiological—winded by their troubles, they focused on their next breath.

For Ramban, it means shortness of perspective. People in trouble lose their ability to hope for or believe in a better future. In their despondence, the Jews could not internalize Moses' promise of a better future.

Sforno reads the word for "spirit" as "faith in Hashem." Four times in the space of two verses, Sforno uses the verb בינה, as in להתבונן, "to think through carefully, to come to understand fully." They didn't believe Moses because they failed to think it through, and they did not see the truth he was presenting. He identifies this lack of faith as the reason they did not merit entering the Land of Israel.

Since the Torah says explicitly that that generation was kept out of Israel because of the sin of the spies, Sforno's different reason seems to mean that the lack of faith they demonstrated here led to them not believing the spies either. Or perhaps that had they disciplined themselves to believe in Moses *here*, they would have had the fiber to reject the pessimism of the spies.

The Elders' Road not Taken on the Path to Redemption

Exod. 5:1 speaks of Moses and Aaron arriving alone at the audience with Pharaoh, even though they had just been speaking with the elders of the people. Rashi assumes the elders started with them but peeled off, one by one, out of fear. At Sinai, Hashem required them to peel off as well, as punishment.

Had they gone to Pharaoh's palace, perhaps a group would have ascended Sinai, instead of Moses alone, with the elders closer to or even on Sinai itself. We'll never know the positive ripples that might have had, but one easy place to think about it is how it might have affected events at the sin of the Golden Calf.

Had the elders been allowed to go as far toward Sinai as Aaron, would they have joined him in arguing with those who doubted Moses' return and demanded a new leader? Would Aaron have had allies other than Hur, per *Chazal*, whom the people killed? Were more of the nation's leaders to have opposed making the Calf, that might have ameliorated or avoided that stain on our national record.

Commentators are prepared to say the Jews could have avoided slavery, could have brought their redemption earlier, could have made it better once it started. Lack of faith drags any redemptive process, even one that ended as well as the Exodus.

We'll never know exactly how, but by pondering it, we can hope to be ready to handle next time better. As we watch this movie annually, we might try this time around to free ourselves of these national flaws.

Perhaps, though, these are the wrong flaws to notice, since they were so early in the process. Perhaps it is unfair to expect slaves to do any better. Tomorrow, we'll look at the later stages of the Exodus, when the plagues had given the Jews significant time to adjust. Sadly, we will see that the failures continued, even after they left Egypt.

Failures on the Eve of Exodus and Its Aftermath

What does it take to change a mindset? Commentators saw the Jews as clinging to their connection to Egypt and the Egyptians, to their accustomed ways of looking at the world, displaying a remarkable resistance to learning from what they were seeing.

I emphasize that I bring this up as a mirror, not to judge them. Their example can help us ready ourselves to react better should we meet parallel situations in the future.

The Jews' Attachment to Egypt

Rashi records the tradition that during the plague of darkness Hashem killed the Jews who were not going to be redeemed (on Exod. 10:22). His sources do not give a reason those Jews were left behind, but Rashi ascribes it to their not wanting to go. In his view, anyone willing was taken out, regardless of their other (often significant) sins.

But this tradition says that the overwhelmingly large segment of the people preferred to stay, and they died in darkness. Rashi at the beginning of *Beshallach* cites the view that eighty percent were blind to Moses' message; the Midrash itself has views that it was a higher percentage than that.

I read this as a reminder that Jews have always developed excessive attachments to where they live, often in spite of significant hardships. *Chazal* and Rashi had no problem saying that most Jews, with all the troubles of slavery, wanted to stay. Unless they assumed the Jews of Egypt differed radically from the Jews they knew, they seem to be signaling their impression that their fellow Jews, in the times of *Chazal* and of Rashi, would also prefer where they were living to going to Israel.

Thoughout history, only a small percentage of Jews has been ready to uproot themselves and head to Israel when the opportunity arises. Most have to be dragged or pushed out.

The Forgotten Holocaust of Egypt

Many of us have heard of this tradition of Jews' dying in the plague of darkness, but I wonder whether we stop to note that it means *Chazal* thought of the generation that left Egypt as survivors of a devastation worse (in percentage killed) than the Holocaust. I stress that we need not claim that this is historical fact, or that *Chazal* meant it that way, for the lessons to be worth learning. Regardless of what actually happened in Egypt, *Chazal* found it plausible that well more than three quarters of the Jewish people were left behind.

The destruction they contemplated was also more sudden than the Holocaust. In their reading, the joy of the Exodus would surely have been tempered with the sorrow of loss, since everyone who left would have known someone killed. For *Chazal,* the Jews of the desert had to balance survivorship with their participation in a great redemption, not all that different from the European Jews who moved to Israel and saw the establishment of the State of Israel in 1948.

The Jews' Strong Bonds with Egyptians

In another example of tradition's seeing the Jews as having become overly enmeshed in Egyptian society, Rashi (on Exod. 12:12-13) notes *Chazal's* inference that foreign first-born in Egypt, Egyptian first-born abroad, and Egyptian first-born in Jews' houses would all be killed (but not Jewish first-born found in Egyptian houses).

I find it surprising that *Chazal* thought Jewish first-born would spend that night in Egyptian homes, and vice versa. We often think slavery divides slave and master, but comments like these (and the text itself, such as when the Jews ask their *neighbors* for gold and silver) assume that some members of these two nations got along well.

Our tradition is teaching us that there was a strong bond between the Egyptians and the Jews. This is despite the fact that these were the Jews who had survived the plague of darkness, proving (in *Chazal's* reading) that they were part of a tiny minority willing to follow Moses out of Egypt, and despite hundreds of years of slavery that preceded the Exodus.

Delaying War

The first verse of *Beshallach* (Exod. 13:17) tells of Hashem's decision to take the Jews through the desert, to avoid the Jews' reacting badly to a war so soon after becoming free. Ramban explains that the desert road would delay war until they were too far to contemplate returning to Egypt, to improve the odds they would handle it well. Rashi points out that even on the longer route, the spies' report of their need to fight their way into Israel led some to argue exactly what Hashem here explicitly hoped to avoid, a desire to return to Egypt.

Even with all of Hashem's assistance, all the plagues and other miracles the Jews had seen, they were still unable or unready to understand what they should have, that they could win any war with Hashem's help. Believing that would have meant abandoning the knowledge that in war, the stronger nation wins; with all they had seen, they could not take that next step to understand that once Hashem becomes directly involved, literally anything can happen.

Taking Time to Be Ready for the Torah

The *Kli Yakar* thinks Hashem took the Jews the long way because they were not yet worthy of receiving the Torah. Their time was designed to teach them הסתפקות, the idea of being satisfied with what one has. The miracles were designed to instill the Jews with faith.

That explains the verses' referring to the Jews as העם, "the nation" several times. Upon leaving Egypt, they did not have the requisite faith and were also unwilling to live within their means, always searching for more wealth and luxury (another theme the *Kli Yakar* seems to be translating from his time back to the Torah's time). The miracles of the Red Sea and Hashem's sustaining them in the desert taught them the necessary lessons to become בני ישראל, the Jewish people.

The *Kli Yakar* also raises the possibility that the word העם, "the nation" refers to the ערב רב, the Egyptian hangers-on who joined the Jews. While earlier he spoke approvingly of their willingness to defy Pharaoh, here and at the Sea he sees them as lacking faith. *They* were the ones unready to face an army, the ones who complained at the Sea, in this reading.

Meaning that, in his view, one can demonstrate much faith and commitment and yet not have reached the necessary minimum expected of a Jew.

Armed or Not

The Torah tells us the Jews were חמושים when they left Egypt. The simplest meaning is that they were armed, explaining in advance how they had weapons for later battles. But it also draws our attention to their timidity.

Ramban says the weapons were actually a symptom of their inability to rely on Hashem's help. Soon after, at Exod. 14:8, Ramban reads the verse's description of the Jews leaving ביד רמה, "with a strong hand," as saying they walked confidently and securely into their future, having left behind their slave's sense of limited options, without commenting on the change. Somewhere in this process, for Ramban, the Jews achieved the proper confidence that Hashem would help them reach their best possible future.

The Terror of Flight

The *Yerushalmi*, cited by the *Torah Temimah* (Exod. 14:10-12), says that when the Jews saw the Egyptians chasing them, they broke into four groups, none of which behaved as it should have.

The *Kli Yakar* suggests that the Jews doubted Moses, not Hashem. They assumed that had Hashem brought them there, Pharaoh would not be chasing them (reminding us that we can think we know what Hashem will do, and be completely wrong). Pursuing the distinction between בני ישראל and עם he made before, the *Kli Yakar* suggests the born Jews (*Benei Yisrael*) had full faith, but the ערב רב, the Egyptians who had latched on, questioned what was happening and complained about leaving.

To highlight the internal divisions, the *Kli Yakar* reads "neither coming close to the other all night" (Exod. 14:2) as referring to the Jews themselves, who were unable to bridge the gaps among them.

He sees that same division in the two ways the verse speaks of the experience of walking through the Sea. Verse 22 says they came into the Sea on dry land, while 29 changes that to walking on dry land in the midst of the Sea. The first refers to those of faith, who went into the water before it split, while the second to those who waited until it had split before moving forward.

Even After the Sea

On verse 30, Rashi notes the tradition that, after the Egyptians drowned in the Sea, their bodies washed up on the shore so that the Jews couldn't claim the Egyptians escaped safely on the other side, as the Jews had emerged on their side.

It sounds easy to believe in Hashem after having witnessed the ten plagues, having had Hashem personally take us out of Egypt, split the Sea for us, lead us through it on dry land, and provide us with food. However, Rabbinic tradition assumes that the Jews struggled to adjust their thinking and their expectations to the new reality they were being shown. Many failed. Some couldn't take the first step, some couldn't navigate change at the pace Hashem demanded. Watching their mistakes, working to relive their experience, we can and should use this to chart a better path.

But perhaps our own forefathers' failings are too sensitive a topic, carry too much of a whiff of the judgmental. We'll have it easier with the Egyptians, to whom we have no loyalty. Sadly, we might find that even their failures are ones we could see ourselves committing.

The Egyptians Could Have Done Better

The Torah makes Pharaoh the foil to Moses and Aaron, mentioning the Egyptian people only infrequently. This can give the impression that they were pawns of their evil king, suffering for something beyond their control. Ramban and others—who lived under monarchs, so we'd have expected them to see how impossible it is to resist a tyrant—reject that perspective, adding the Egyptian populace to our growing list of those who teach us by making mistakes we can avoid.

Ramban on Limited Monarchy
and the Guilt of Egyptian Civilians

At the start of the book of Exodus, Ramban claims Pharaoh wanted to kill the Jews right away, but the Egyptian people would not stomach unjustified murder. Opting for stealthier means, he started with slavery, which he phrased as a tax of servitude, aimed at all non-citizens. When that didn't work, he secretly ordered the midwives to kill male babies in childbirth. After they found ways to circumvent that decree, Pharaoh switched to more active ways of killing.

Even there, Ramban claims, people would not tolerate the palace endorsing such actions. Pharaoh had to let word out, unattached to his name, that anyone who threw male Jewish babies in the river would not be prosecuted. Lifting the protection of law sufficed for rank-and-file Egyptians to choose murder. Yet when it became known Pharaoh had been behind it, in Ramban's view, enough Egyptians objected that he had to put a stop to it.

Ramban gives more power to the people than we might have expected. At each stage, in his view, had they stood firmly against Pharaoh, he would have had to back down (and sometimes in fact he did). With power comes responsibility; knowing they could have stopped their king, we are faced with the ramifications of where they did not.

According to Ramban's reading, many Egyptians had no moral qualms about killing Jews, and all or close to all willingly joined Pharaoh in enslaving them. Even their opposition to some of Pharaoh's decrees was, for Ramban, more political prudence than moral conviction. Ceding the king's right to wipe out one population without cause would establish a precedent that could backfire.

Lack of political power is one kind of problem, lack of the sense of right and wrong that leads to protest is another, and joining in some of the ruler's evils is yet another. The Egyptians were already presenting themselves poorly.

The Sequence of the Plagues, Ramban and Ibn Ezra's View

Ramban argues that Moses was sent to meet Pharaoh at the water before the plagues of blood, wild animals, and hail—

the deadliest plagues—to be sure the Egyptian people heard the warning as well as Pharaoh. This is in contrast to *Chazal's* idea that Pharaoh went to the river to relieve himself in private, part of maintaining an image of himself as a god.

Ramban thinks instead that the king going to the waters would have involved a large entourage. Because the coming plague would be extraordinarily destructive, the people were included, to give them a chance to pressure Pharaoh to concede. Their refraining, Ramban adds, made them culpable themselves.

Ramban's sequence seems to be: a catastrophic plague preceded by a national warning, a slightly less damaging one with in-palace notification, and the third with no advance word and no loss of life. Almost like an earthquake, each aftershock diminishing in force but a reminder of the original, with the looming threat of another on the horizon.

In addition to repeating his assumption that public pressure could and did change the course of events, he states more explicitly his view that the people were liable for not protesting. Today, many people deny both that ordinary citizens have the power to force their leaders' hands (especially when the leaders are despots), and that the failure to use that power makes them somewhat complicit.

Where do we stand on speaking up about that which is wrong or evil around us? If we allow ourselves to stay silent, do we feel we have accepted some of the responsibility for what comes next?

The Frogs: Making It Worse

Rashi offers two readings of the plague of the frogs. In the second, he quotes a tradition that one large frog came out of the river, and as the Egyptians hit the giant animal, it shot out streams of smaller frogs. Textually, the Midrash is building off a quirk of Biblical Hebrew, which can use a singular to indicate a group; here, the Torah speaks of הצפרדע, literally "the frog," singular, rising up over Egypt.

Whatever the derivation, the image is of a plague that would have been less severe had the people left it alone. Had they only stopped hitting it after the first or second time that it shot out more frogs, things wouldn't have gotten as bad as they did.

The Midrash seems to me to imply that the Egyptians insisted they could figure out how to handle this, as they did during the plague of blood, digging around the river for water (Exod. 7:24). Their self-defeating arrogance led them to decide the plagues were an engineering problem to be tackled, finding alternate water sources for the blood, and a way to kill the frogs.

They never found their way to the solution staring them in the face: submitting to Hashem's Will and forcing Pharaoh to release the Jews. Perhaps one step more realistic is that they never found their way to asking Moses, sincerely, what they should do. All the way at the end of the process, when the first-born were dying, Pharaoh told the Jews to leave, but neither he nor his people could ever bring themselves to ask Moses what their best reaction would be.

Failing to Notice the Death of the Jews in Darkness

We have already discussed the tradition that Jews were killed during darkness. According to Rashi (Exod. 10:22), Hashem killed them in that plague so the Egyptians would not know about it. Had the Egyptians been aware that Jews were dying as well, they would have used it to convince themselves it wasn't the Jews' God bringing these plagues.

It takes a certain blindness to see a bunch of Jews die and not notice that it was a specific population, those who had refused to leave Egypt when Hashem called for them to go. They're also seen as blind to the fact that only twenty percent of the Jews were left after the plague of darkness. *Chazal* think that its having happened when they couldn't see it would have been enough for them not to notice. Perhaps they were preoccupied with their own troubles, which were about to worsen. Or perhaps another of their flaws was that they only saw what affected their immediate interests.

But the blindness I find most interesting is the one that would allow them to fasten on the one fact that many Jews were killed in darkness as proof it wasn't the Jews' God bringing all this on them. With all the signs offered, the plagues being predicted and ended on demand, with the Jews spared from all those, Jews' dying during a plague when Egyptians *weren't* dying would have let them insist this couldn't be Hashem.

Laying a Trap for Pharaoh

When Hashem tells Moses to have the Jews travel back and camp in front of בעל צפון, Baal Tsefon, Rashi says this would mislead Pharaoh into thinking the Jews were lost and therefore vulnerable. Tradition had it that this was also the only idol left after the Exodus; seeing the Jews stumble into its territory, the Egyptians could fool themselves into thinking this idol had power over them.

Sforno thinks Hashem expected the Egyptians to assume Baal Tsefon had closed the desert on the Jews, and to bemoan their failure to seek help from it earlier. The *Kli Yakar* adds that they had always seen this as the god of gold and silver, who would take umbrage at Hashem's having let the Jews plunder the Egyptians' gold and silver, and would now help overcome Hashem and the Jews.

For all that they had been brought low slowly and methodically, stripped of all assumptions and arrogance, three days later they were ready to fool themselves right back to where they started. Faith can be fragile, ours no less than theirs.

Leaving on Good Terms

When the Jews asked the Egyptians for their gold and silver (Exod. 12:36), the verse says that Hashem put the people's favor into the Egyptians eyes; Ramban takes their readily handing over their prized possessions as showing that they looked well upon the Jews and Moses, that they understood they had been wrong to treat the Jews as they had, and acknowledged the Jews' worthiness of being chosen as Hashem's nation.

It didn't last, as we see at the Sea. Watching the Exodus, we see how the Egyptians could have done more than they recognized to avert their own downfall. They were too willing to tolerate immorality without protest (and, sometimes, they actively participated); they continued to be certain they knew how to handle what came their way, even when they manifestly did not; and, even when dragged to certain truths, they were always ready to seize the slightest counterevidence to regress to their old way of seeing the world.

In building our picture of who we would have been in the Exodus, we have one more reminder of mistakes to avoid. But the best (and final) teacher in that regard is Pharaoh, to whom we turn next.

Pharaoh Takes Himself to His Doom

Caricaturing Pharaoh is the lazy way out. Overhastily assuring ourselves we would never do what he did makes him not worthy of our serious thought. Except that the Torah found him worthy of it, suggesting he bears a closer look.

We find that two of his prominent flaws challenge most of us or those we know and love. He is arrogant, and refuses to (or cannot) change when necessary. Watching where that leads him should remind us to redouble our efforts to avoid his errors, or even do the opposite, and reach great success.

The God Pharaoh Could Not Accept

The first time they speak to Pharaoh, Moses and Aaron refer to Hashem with two different Names. In Exod. 5:1, they call Him א-לקי ישראל, "the God of Israel," and in Exod. 5:3, they call him א-לקי העברים, "the God of the Hebrews." Ramban attributes the change to Pharaoh's inability to assimilate that first term. Pharaoh knew of א-לקים, a generic or universal God, either because all sophisticated people did or because he knew the story of Joseph.

To accept the more direct Divine Providence indicated by the four-letter Name, or the idea of an א-לקי ישראל, a universal God with a special connection to a particular people, was too much. Realizing they had gone too far, Moses and Aaron adjusted their vocabulary, letting Pharaoh hear it as their national god, a familiar idea.

Sforno thinks Pharaoh rejected the idea of a Creator *ex nihilo*, a Creator of the universe from absolute nothingness. For all that many people believe in gods, or even one God, the claim that that God created everything, including what we call the laws of Nature (and therefore can abrogate or change those), has divided believing Jews from others (even putative monotheists) for millennia.

Both types of denial are present and prominent today, meaning that if prophets made the same claims Ramban and Sforno think Moses and Aaron did, they might be met with the same reaction. As it was then, so we could imagine it being now, easing our way to turning our retelling into a reliving.

Part of our human responsibility—true for the Jews in Egypt, true for Pharaoh, true for us—is recognizing Hashem as Hashem presents Himself, not insisting we can define or set limits on what Hashem can be. Pharaoh could not believe in a God Who had a special connection with the Jewish people, or a Creator of something from nothing. Today, too, many say, "The God I believe in would never..." setting rules and limits for God, shaping Hashem in their image.

Foreshadowing the Killing of the First-Born

In that same first conversation, Exod. 4:22, Moses relays Hashem's message that the Jews are His first-born, as it were.

Should Pharaoh refuse to release them, Hashem will kill *his* first-born (a warning repeated again before the plague of hail, according to Rashi). Pharaoh rejects the idea, and the first-born eventually are killed. Once it happens, does he recall that he had been put on notice back at the beginning of the process, that these deaths should not be shocking?

It seems likely Pharaoh did not or could not absorb Moses' framework for the events coming his way. Watching him, we can wonder whether we are more open to Hashem's messages, better able to hear divine calls to grow in unexpected directions, or even to see where challenges that come our way are punishment.

We have it harder, because we don't have a prophet telling us which events are directly orchestrated by Hashem or what they mean. Pharaoh's story suggests that's not always what makes us refuse to see Hashem's hand in events. Sometimes we reject the truth even when a Moses tells it to us directly.

Easing Pharaoh's Path to
Acceptance: The Role of a Prophet?

Hashem says that Moses will be an *Elohim* over Pharaoh, and Aaron will be a *navi* to Moses (Exod. 76:1). Rashi there explains Aaron's role as follows: ימליצנו ויטעימנו, Aaron will make the words sound commendable and reasonable to Pharaoh. Aaron is to shape the words of Moses into a message that Pharaoh would be most likely to receive.

Empowering Aaron in this way implies an interest in helping Pharaoh respond in the best way possible (similar to Sforno's claim that the first nine plagues were spurs to repentance). Moses heard Hashem's messages in full; Pharaoh heard Aaron's more easily digested presentations (and *still* rejected them).

Rashi on Hashem's Hardening Pharaoh's Heart

Rashi's sense that Aaron's job was to present the words more appealingly does not correspond with Hashem's telling Moses that He will harden Pharaoh's heart. Rashi does not address the discrepancy, but three of his points about the hardening clarify his view.

In Exod. 7:3, Rashi understands Hashem to be telling Moses that non-Jews never pay the kind of full attention necessary to penitence. Because of that, Hashem will harden Pharaoh's heart to let the plagues continue. Had Pharaoh "surprised" Hashem by achieving the required level of contrition, the plagues might have ended earlier.

Rashi's second point is that Hashem punishes idolaters to educate Jews. I have seen those who understand this to mean those other nations are a tool to teach the Jews a lesson, but I believe Rashi means that *since* Pharaoh deserves all this punishment and more, Hashem will harden his heart to make sure the Jews fully learn the necessary lesson. Repentance might have avoided the punishment, but his deeds made it already deserved.

Finally, Rashi notes that the verse only says Hashem directly hardens Pharaoh's heart starting with the sixth plague. This fits with Rambam's claim that Pharaoh's initial persecution of the Jews lost him his free will (*Teshuvah* 6:3).

According to Rashi, Pharaoh was not encouraged to do anything he did not want nor did he suffer anything he did not previously deserve. He and the Egyptians could have repented as long as they did so sincerely and fully. What Hashem prevented was their paying lip service to yielding, without the internal conversion that had to go with it.

As Free Will Ebbs Away, Piling Up Bad Decisions

Pharaoh was not killed with the other first-born. According to Rashi, that was so he would witness the drama at the Sea. He does not explain why Hashem would want Pharaoh to witness the destruction at the Red Sea, especially if Pharaoh has already lost his free will.

One possibility is that others would be more impressed with the Splitting of the Sea if they knew Pharaoh had been there. It seems to me that Hashem might have only hardened his heart in the one area of freeing the Jews before the plagues were done, or before he chased them to the Sea. In other areas, Pharaoh might have had free will, and he might have used it to moderate his evil behavior.

The Moment of Freedom

In Exod. 10:28-29, Pharaoh and Moses have a heated exchange, whose outcome is that Moses says he will never again see Pharaoh's face. In Exod. 12:31-2, after the death of the first-born, Pharaoh begs Moses to take the Jews and leave, which seems like they are speaking face to face. Rashi solves the problem by saying that Moses only said that he would never again initiate a meeting. Here, Pharaoh initiated contact.

Ramban offers three other options: (1) Pharaoh did not see Moses and Aaron that night—he ran to their house, cried out in the darkness for them to leave, and they never opened the door; (2) Pharaoh sent a messenger, even though the text seems to indicate that Moses and Pharaoh spoke directly; (3) Moses only meant he would never speak to Pharaoh in his palace again.

Three options for how Pharaoh surrendered. His desperate banging, calling for them to leave without them even answering, evinces a more complete yielding. Especially if he has the calm to entrust the mission to a messenger, but even if he went himself but made sure to include his entourage, the second two options show him holding fast to a shred of his remaining dignity, which would explain his next choices.

Ready to Be Fooled into Trying Again

Sforno rejects the literal meaning of Exod. 13:17, that Hashem only didn't take the Jews by way of the Philistines because of how they'd react to war. Since Mt. Sinai is not on that route, and Hashem had already told Moses that the Jews would receive the Torah there, they had to get to Sinai. Sforno instead understands the verse to say that Hashem took the Jews into the desert to lure Pharaoh and the Egyptians to their destruction. Because as soon as Pharaoh saw the Jews were lost, he would give chase, despite the plagues he and his people had suffered.

We've already seen a similar idea in Rashi's reading of Hashem telling Moses to have the Jews camp in front of בעל צפון, Baal Tsefon (Exod. 14:2), a ploy to mislead Pharaoh and the Egyptians into thinking the Jews were vulnerable.

It's one last opportunity to question ourselves and whether, when, and how we learn lessons we need. Do we resist them or embrace them? When do we resist, when do we give up? Once learned, how fragile are those lessons, how easily can they be unlearned?

Pharaoh is a model of what we want to avoid.

Which leaves us only one day until the Seder. My hope is that our review of how Hashem invites our participation in our redemption and how the major characters in the Exodus succeeded and failed at taking advantage of those opportunities has readied us to experience the Seder fully, to relive the Exodus as much as possible.

What we haven't yet done is directly connect our discussions here to the flow of the Seder story told in the Haggadah. That's the second part of this book, *My Father's Seder, Foundation of My Faith,* a memoir of how my father turned the Seder into an opportunity to communicate life-values, faith, and religious devotion and connection, within an atmosphere of fun and celebration.

For us, though, we can turn to the next piece of this endeavor, starting to see how the Exodus that we will relive Seder night impacts our lives the rest of the year.

Pesach All Year: Unexpected
Mitzvot of Remembering Egypt

It doesn't take much education to know Jews are supposed
to remember the Exodus—we have the holiday of Pesach,
which includes specific obligations to remind us of the events,
such as telling the story at length Seder night, and avoiding
leavened bread and eating matzah for seven days. Shabbat
and the other major holidays also specifically commemorate
the Exodus; and we have *Zechirat Yetziat Mitzrayim*, a twice-
daily obligation to recall the Exodus in Shema.

With the Seder looming, we can begin to realize that
what happens at the Seder is meant to spread into the
rest of our lives. The rest of this part of the book reviews
commandments the Torah seems to connect to the Exodus.
The Talmud (*Bava Metzia* 61b) records that Rava already
pointed out three such *mitzvot*, wondering why the Torah
links the usury prohibitions, the commandment to wear
tzitzit, and the obligation of honest weights and measures to
the Exodus.

We'll get to his answer, but I start by pointing out
that we can ask that question more systematically—in *all*

mitzvot other than the obvious ones, when and why does the Torah mention Egypt? What does that tell us about the role our nation's founding experiences are supposed to play in our lives?

Establishing God

The first example makes a point about our relationship with Hashem that I think is often missed. In the first of the *Aseret ha-Dibberot*, the Ten Pronouncements we heard at Sinai, Hashem introduces Himself, as it were, with the words, "I am the Lord your God, Who took you out of Egypt out of the land of slavery."

Why make that the reference point—isn't it more significant that Hashem created the Universe? The obvious but important answer is that the Torah is purposely making the Exodus central to how we think of Hashem. While Hashem *is* Creator of the Universe (vital to other faith issues, such as the belief in miracles), for Jews, He is—more importantly—He Who took us out of Egypt.

Rashi writes that the taking out is the sufficient cause of our eternal obligation to obey Hashem completely. We don't keep the Torah because the Creator commands it; we do it out of a sense of personal and national debt, extending back to Egypt.

Experience Is Better Than Reports, and What an Experience

Two later commentators, R. Yehudah b. Eliezer of the early fourteenth century and the *Kli Yakar* in the sixteenth, assumed Hashem referred to the Exodus because it was more immediate, in that these Jews had themselves seen it. Our relationship with Hashem isn't with a distant or aloof Creator, it's an answer to the call of the Protector Who took us out of slavery and oppression.

Ramban and Rambam agree that this first Pronouncement establishes a *mitzvah*. Just as a Jew has to say *Kiddush* on Shabbat, know Torah and teach it to his sons, remember the Exodus story, and more, there is a specific obligation on all Jews, male or female, to know and believe in the Redeemer Who took us from Egypt.

God is a word used loosely today. Ramban gives a basic definition: the God Jews must believe in, he says, pre-existed the world (and thus is "able" to violate the laws of Nature, not just manipulate them), created the world intentionally and deliberately (not as some involuntary outpouring, as Aristotle seems to assume), and is involved with the world, as shown by choosing the Jewish people, extricating them from Egypt with great miracles, and forming a lasting covenant with them.

Sforno echoes some of this. For him and Ramban, the Exodus was an historical demonstration of Hashem's presence and power, intentionally and explicitly to teach an eternal lesson. All who saw the Exodus were supposed to have had their doubts erased, forever, on issues that some people today try to dismiss as philosophical nuances.

A Life of Servitude to Hashem

R. Samson Raphael Hirsch, writing in the nineteenth century, takes that another step, as relevant today as when he wrote it. This Pronouncement isn't interested in *whether* to believe, he says, because Judaism doesn't look for a philosophical declaration of faith, even faith in a particular version of Hashem (such as One vs. many).

The key point of Jewish faith, and of this Pronouncement, is that the one and unitary Hashem is *my* Hashem, Who shaped and formed *me*, obligated me, and continues to be involved in the course of my life. The Exodus taught that what happens to Jews, from Egypt forward, is in some sense directly from Hashem. That personal connection is what this statement of Jewish faith means to stress.

R. Hirsch's words have more than a whiff of a reaction to the clockwork universe suggested by Newtonian physics, and the random evolution posited by Darwin. We could take all that out, though, and still have an important point—while many of us get caught up in the yes/no question of God's existence, R. Hirsch is reminding us that that wasn't supposed to be an issue, because Egypt, the memory of which we are tasked with keeping alive, made clear that the right question is, "What does the Hashem with Whom I have a relationship going back to Egypt want me to do?"

The Necessity of the Exodus

An *aggadic* section of *Shabbat* 85b brings these points together in a thought provoking manner. The Gemara tells of Moses ascending to receive the Torah, only to find the angels protesting Hashem's giving such a holy possession to such unworthy recipients. Moses is called to respond, and he notes the mention of the Exodus in the first Pronouncement, and asks the angels, "Were you slaves to Pharaoh? Were you redeemed by Hashem? Then for what do you need the Torah?"

That implies that the value of Torah depends on having been in Egypt and been taken out, when many of us assume that Torah is valuable for the eternal verities it proclaims. As if—similar to R. Hirsch—we aren't required to act certain ways because Hashem created the world. We're required to act those ways because Hashem saved us from Egypt. For angels, who did not experience Hashem's salvation, the Torah is irrelevant.

(As an important aside, Ramban understands there to be a Biblical prohibition against forgetting Hashem, Who took us out of Egypt, as well as a positive commandment to remember.)

Not bad for a start on seeing where the Exodus plays a role beyond the narrow confines of Pesach and related observances. Where else is it important?

Tefillin, a Two-Purposed Mitzvah

The Torah speaks about *tefillin* four times, once in each of the four Biblical sections we include in the boxes we wear on our arms and heads. Two of those are in the first paragraphs of Shema, where *tefillin* are mentioned as a written reminder of Torah and *mitzvot* generally.

Exodus 13 refers to *tefillin* twice in the context of the Paschal sacrifice and the offering of first-borns to Hashem. In each case, the discussion closes by saying we should keep them as a sign, on our arms and heads, that Hashem took us out of Egypt with a mighty hand. The first instance (Exod. 13:9) leaves some room to be read as being about Torah in general. Ramban explains that placing the memory of the Exodus on our arms and heads reminds us of what Hashem did for us, stimulating us to always have Torah and *mitzvot* in our mouths.

In line with his discussion of the first Pronouncement, R. Samson Raphael Hirsch sees *tefillin* as a symbol of our acknowledgement that we have to cede our existence and all our desires to Hashem, with all our hearts, and have to pass that message to our children as well.

The mentions of the Exodus in the context of *tefillin* thus seem to locate our awareness of Torah and *mitzvot* in the experience of the Exodus. Sure, *tefillin* are about remembering Torah and *mitzvot* in general, and our obligation to keep them. But the verses in Exodus 13 tell us that one of the ways *tefillin* draws our attention to those big ideas is by focusing us on what we might make the mistake of thinking of as a small idea, the Exodus.

Tzitzit

We include the verse that connects *tzitzit* to the Exodus in our twice-daily recitation of Shema. The *Tur, Orach Chayyim* 8, asserts that this needs focused intent, even more than other *mitzvot*. The *Bach* suggests that he derived that from the

Torah's giving a reason for our observance. When the Torah says we wear *tefillin* "so that" we remember the Exodus, the *Tur* thought it mandated extra focus. That would mean that, for *tzitzit*, a central goal of the wearing is to keep us in mind of the Exodus. All day, as a Jew looks at his garments and notices strings attached, it should remind him of the Exodus.

The *Sifrei*, the *Midrash Halachah* to *Bamidbar* (*halachically* authoritative in the absence of contradictory Talmudic evidence), offers etymologies for two *tzitzit*-related terms that conspicuously tie them to the Exodus. First, R. Shimon b. Elazar asks why the color of the non-white string is named *techelet*, answering that it's because the Egyptians' first-born נתכלו, "were diminished." Alternatively, it's because the Egyptians themselves כלו, "were destroyed," at the Sea.

The *Sifrei* relates the word *tzitzit* itself to Hashem's peeking inside the Jews' homes in Egypt, based on Song of Songs 2:8-9, which speaks of the beloved (Hashem) looking through the windows, peeking, מציץ, "through the lattices."

In other words, this *Sifrei* reads the two main words characterizing this garment as putting us back in the Egypt experience: one as a reminder of Hashem's destroying our enemies, either through their first born or all of them, the other of Hashem's watching over us, always alert to our need for assistance and/or salvation.

With just three *mitzvot*, and twenty to come, we already see that there's more to the role the Exodus plays in our Jewish lives than we sometimes remember to remember.

Sanctifying (or Profaning)
Hashem's Name, Prophesying in
the Name of Idolatry as Exodus-Related Issues

In Lev. 22:32, the Torah warns us against profaning Hashem's Name, and tells us that that Name must be sanctified among the Jewish people. (I write it that way because the Torah uses a passive verb, perhaps because the starkest case is allowing ourselves to be killed rather than violate the Torah. More below.) Hashem then declares, "I am the One Who sanctifies you."

As stated, this seems a perfectly formed mitzvah, no obvious holes in its presentation. Hashem sanctified us with Torah and *mitzvot,* included in which are these two obligations. Yet in the next verse, the Torah adds that Hashem took us out of Egypt to be our Lord.

What does that add to our understanding? To answer, we have to define these commandments a little more fully. While the verse puts the prohibition first, it's easier to speak about the obligation to sanctify.

Sanctifying Hashem's Name—the Extreme Version
Rashi in Leviticus already mentions perhaps the most well-known aspect of the mitzvah, which is that Jews are

sometimes obligated to die rather than transgress the Torah. At the strictest level, Jews are obligated to die rather than commit alien worship, murder, or sexual immorality. That requirement extends to *any* commandment that has become the target of specific religious attack. The term in Hebrew is שמד, *shemad*, an attempt to destroy the Jewish religion, but it doesn't have to be aimed at the whole religion—any element that comes under specific attack becomes a point of שמד, and our obligation to avoid transgressing it is then heightened by the need to sanctify Hashem's Name.

It's hard to offer unequivocal examples, but if a country or municipality were to decide that religious objections to eating non-kosher meat were unacceptable, and to coerce the eating of such meat, Jews would plausibly be obligated to refuse, even at the cost of their lives (which is not true, for example, if that government decided to require eating that meat for other reasons).

We are obligated to dig in our heels in the face of specific attacks on our religion, with the same stubbornness as we always have to show over murder, sexual improprieties, or alien worship. To understand why, let's look at an everyday (and more pleasant) version of the mitzvah.

Sanctifying Hashem's Name Daily

A Mishnah in *Megillah* 23b lists ceremonies that require the presence of a *minyan*, a quorum of ten male Jews. These include saying *Barechu*, *Kedushah* in the repetition of the

Amidah, the priestly blessings, reading the Torah and/or *haftarah*, and *sheva brachot* in celebration of a wedding

The Gemara cites our verse, which says that sanctifying the Name is בתוך בני ישראל, "among the Jewish people." Since these ceremonies are *devarim she-bi-kedushah*, matters of sanctity, they must be enacted among the Jewish people, like the more formal *kiddush Hashem*. A *minyan* is the smallest representative grouping of the entire people.

Rambam's formulation of the commandment (*Sefer ha-Mitzvot*, Positive Commandment 9) explains how both can be matters of *kiddush Hashem*. He renders the commandments as being to "publicize this true faith in the world, and not fear injury (or damage) from any injurer (source of damage)." Mostly, we publicize this faith by announcing Hashem's Presence, such as when the community performs the various *devarim she-bi-kedushah*. But when an oppressor comes, we cannot allow the impression that pressure could ever lead us to deny Hashem or any of His *mitzvot*.

The Exodus Component

As defined so far, however, it's not clear why this is limited to Jews. Why shouldn't non-Jews have to resist an oppressor's attempts to make them violate the Noahide laws? Why may they yield to the duress of transgressing serious sins?

The *Sifra* (*Emor* 9) points to the verse's mention of the Exodus for the answer. Non-Jews do not have to forfeit their lives in Hashem's Name because they weren't taken out of Egypt. Part of Hashem's taking us out, according to the *Sifra*, was that it made us the nation who would sanctify His Name by spreading word of it and by holding fast to our adherence to Hashem's commands, even in the face of death.

That the Exodus made it our responsibility to represent Hashem also explains the other side of this mitzvah, the prohibition of profaning Hashem's Name.

Three Versions of *Chillul Hashem*

When I was a child, adults spoke of חילול ה', profaning Hashem's Name, any time a Jew embarrassed the religion (like when boys wearing *kippot* were too noisy on a subway). This rationale was based on the relationship between *kiddush* and *chillul*—if *kiddush* is about announcing Hashem in the world, then *chillul* is failing to represent Him honorably. This is more explicit in Ezekiel 36, in a less *halachic* setting. Rambam makes it clear in our context, noting in *Sefer ha-Mitzvot*, Negative Commandment 63, that the two are opposites; if קידוש ה' is doing our part to declare Hashem's Name, then disgracing that Name is חילול.

The Talmud (*Shabbat* 33a) includes *chillul* in a list of *mitzvot* whose violation brings broad consequences such as rampant wild animals, a plague among domesticated animals, a reduction in human population, and roads becoming deserted. *Chillul Hashem* is also one of the few commandments for which the Talmud (*Yoma* 86a) assumes we can only get full atonement with death.

Rambam shows three ways to commit חילול. First, we might yield to duress when we were supposed to resist. It's not a full violation of the prohibition because it was coerced, but it nonetheless qualifies as a *chillul Hashem.*

Willful or Exemplary Violations of the Torah

Rambam adds that when a Jew violates the Torah for no reason other than to shuck off the yoke of Heaven, that is also a *chillul Hashem.* Walking down the street, a Jew decides to eat a cheeseburger, not out of hunger but to express how chafing he or she finds Torah. That would be a *chillul Hashem* in addition to a full violation of the prohibition. Rashi seems to agree, since he interprets ולא תחללו, "do not profane," as לעבור עליו מזידין, "to transgress purposely." He means, I think, that the person violates for that reason alone, not because of any other urges.

Rambam's third version of חילול is where a notable person acts in ways that give a wrong impression (Rashi writes similarly at *Shabbat* 33a). Rambam's example is from *Yoma* 86a, which says it is a *chillul Hashem* when an important person takes meat without paying for it (in a place where it was uncommon to extend credit), or walking a short distance without either speaking Torah or wearing *tefillin.* Rashi says this type of behavior will teach others to treat Torah and observance lightly—if *that* person doesn't see a reason to be careful, why should I?

The formulation might apply to each of us at our own level. Most of us impact *some* others with our caring for Torah, or lack of it. In those circles, there would seem room to argue that we run the risk of חילול ה' as well, even without committing actual sins. If I am seen as a a paragon of Jewish observance in my place of work, for example, then giving my coworkers the sense that I've treated Torah lightly might also count in these terms of *chillul Hashem*.

That's the subway example—publicly identified Jews represent Hashem's Torah, so even the misbehavior of talking too loudly could profane Hashem's Name in just this way. And, once again, the Torah grounds our responsibility to avoid this on the Exodus, not just an amorphous general obligation we bear towards Hashem.

Prophesying in the Name of Alien Worship

Deut 13:5 closes a discussion of a prophet who promotes alien worship by saying that the prophet should be put to death, because a false prophet has spoken ill of (or, incited rebellion against) Hashem, who took you out of Egypt and redeemed you from slavery. The *Sifrei* notes that that our relationship with Hashem, grounded in the Exodus, should render us immune to the exhortations of such a prophet.

Rambam, Negative Commandment 28, sees that prohibition as extending to even *considering* the prophet's call to alien worship. Ramban seems to agree, because he says that the verse means that Hashem's having performed the miracles in Egypt should mean that we know, for all time, not to worship any god other than Hashem, and thus there could never be a prophecy that would tell us to do so.

The *Sefer ha-Chinuch* 456 follows Rambam in counting a prohibition to even *listen* to the prophet, let alone to follow what such a person says. The *Sefer ha-Chinuch* says the weakness of our intellects, the ease with which someone can mislead us, means we cannot even debate a putative prophet, for fear that such a person will be more convincing than we are—despite prophesying a complete falsehood.

I find the insight of the *Chinuch* particularly interesting in a time when people's confidence (in multiple realms, including Torah) often far outstrips their right to that confidence. A proper humility about our ability, on our own, to recognize truth or falsehood is part of what's necessary to avoid being drawn in by a false prophet, realizing such people can lure us into believing that which is blatantly false. The Exodus was supposed to be a bulwark, shoring up our defenses against any obviously contra-Torah ideas.

Three more ways the experience of Egypt affects our everyday life: the obligation to take our part in a people who sanctify Hashem's Name, in whatever way is called for at that time, the ban on profaning that Name, in any of the various possible ways, and our need to carry the Exodus with us so fully that it makes clear the falsity of any prophet who claims we should worship anything other than Hashem.

Enticing People to Alien Worship as
a Crime Against the Memory of the Exodus

Like yesterday's *mitzvot*, there would be plenty of reason to prohibit a מסית, *mesit*, a Jew who tries to entice another Jew to עבודה זרה, worship anything other than Hashem, without mentioning the Exodus. But the Torah does, so let's see what that tells us about the mitzvah and about the role the Exodus plays in our lives all year round, not just at Pesach time.

We'll start with another noteworthy aspect of this mitzvah—the amount of attention the Torah gives it—and the level of negativity attached to it. From there, I think we'll come to a better understanding of what a *mesit* was, and might be today.

So Many Prohibitions

Deut. 13:17-12 assumes a *mesit* will act in private, with someone they're close to, and the Torah warns us not to listen and not to continue to love or like the inciter. In fact (as Rashi notes and as Rambam includes in *Sefer ha-Mitzvot*), *halachah* understands the Torah to obligate the target of the incitement to *hate* the inciter, prohibits saving the inciter in a perilous situation, prohibits the target/victim from offering reasons to absolve the inciter, and obligates that victim to bring forward any damning evidence he or she knows. In all, Rambam counts six prohibitions, close to two percent of the prohibitions in the Torah.

Remember that the target will have been a close friend or relative of the *mesit*, but the Torah obligates the victim to bring this close friend or relative to court, stay silent about exculpatory aspects of the case, offer all incriminating ones, and, if the court found the person liable, take the lead in administering the death penalty. And there's more.

Subtracting Compassion

Based on the Torah's telling us not to be enamored of nor have compassion for the inciter, the *Sifrei* contrasts the court's conduct in these cases to the usual obligation to love our fellow Jews. Other Jews don't lose their hold on our *halachic* affections when they commit serious sins, but the Torah tells us we must stop loving the inciter. That reveals itself in several oddities in the court procedure for judging this inciter.

Ordinary defendants can expect judges in *halachic* courts to seek out any avenue of leniency in their case (that's why such courts traditionally didn't allow lawyers; it was the judges' obligation to find the truth, and all plausible roads to innocence). The Talmud (*Sanhedrin* 29a) offers a teaching of R. Chiyya b. Abba's—reported by R. Chama bar Chanina—that the court does not do that for an inciter.

Furthermore, similar to double jeopardy, *halachic* courts do not generally reopen acquittals. *Sanhedrin* 33b tells us we *would* reopen a conviction, even if the defendant was on the way to execution; the possibility of avoiding killing an innocent always leads us to reopen the case. For a *mesit*, the reverse is true; once convicted, we don't reopen the case, and we'll reopen an acquittal if new evidence comes to light.

Sanhedrin 36b tells us that eunuchs (who cannot marry), the elderly, and the childless cannot sit on courts, seemingly because we lack confidence that they will bring the proper compassion and empathy to the proceedings. There may be many elderly and childless who are highly empathetic, perhaps more than those who are young and have children, but the Gemara thought it was enough of a possibility that it disqualified judges. In contrast, they can, and are perhaps encouraged to, sit on the court of an inciter.

For a last example, *Sanhedrin* 85b notes that children ordinarily may not serve as the court's agents to administer punishments to their parents. A man may deserve lashes or even death, but his son cannot be the one to administer that proper punishment.

Unless the parent is a *mesit*.

All the Rigor

That is not to say we rush to convict an accused inciter—in terms of testing the witnesses, verifying the facts, being sure of the crime, all the usual strictures apply. One exception is the requirement to warn the inciter of the consequences of what he or she is about to do, which is unnecessary for an inciter, but seems to be for technical reasons too involved to discuss here.

These rules would also seem not to apply to an inciter who did not realize he or she was recommending alien worship—today, many Jews deny that certain religions, philosophies, or worldviews count as idolatry, even if *halachah* says they do.

All that being true, we still treat this sinner differently from all others, bringing to bear remarkably few of the usual ways we have to help defendants avoid the most severe punishments instituted by the Torah. Why is the *mesit* so much worse?

Closeness

I think the answer lies in the relationship that lays the groundwork for the inciting. Deut. 13:7 speaks of a brother, son, daughter, wife (the Torah's phrase is "who rests in your bosom"— a wife with whom we're close, whom we love), or close friend ("who is like your soul") approaching us with the idea of adopting alien worship.

In the Torah's time, as in ours, many people acted within multiple traditions—they might have a serious Shabbat observance and a serious Baal observance (or, today, would respectfully join Buddhist, Catholic, and Jewish ceremonies, seeing them all as spiritual and uplifting).

The incitement, in other words, did not have to ask us to abandon Judaism or Hashem. It could ask us to understand that worshipping *Markolis* by throwing stones at it better aligned us with the forces of war, or that setting up our furniture according to the dictates of Feng Shui allows the spirit of the universe to bring us success.

Our Susceptibility to Basing
Right and Wrong on Our Emotions

Recent decades have given us many examples of how closeness with others can lead to accepting their point of view. In just the last few years, more than one public figure has announced that their position on abortion or euthanasia or homosexual activity changed once they knew someone involved in any of those.

That should be irrelevant to deciding the underlying moral and philosophical questions. All of us act wrongly at times, so the fact that someone close to us is wrong, even deeply wrong, cannot be a surprise. Yet many people let the actions of those closest to them lead them to rethinking their views. They seem to think that if the sin doesn't turn their loved one into a monster, how bad could it be?

To me, that's part of the vigilance the Torah urged. It is relatively easy to reject a straightforward call to abandon deeply held beliefs and commitments. But if a close friend or relative invites us to join a wrong practice, that's harder.

We are being warned, it seems to me, that communities and societies do not always change moralities by reasoning to a well-considered decision. We sometimes abandon our moral standards because we are unwilling to look loved ones in the eye and say, "You're wrong; so wrong that I am, sadly, going to have to bring you to court and take a leading role in seeing that you are prosecuted to the full extent of the law."

Difficult as it is, that's our obligation in these cases.

Egypt?

If you're like me, you haven't noticed anything missing in this conversation. Yet in verse 10, the Torah says the reason to stone this close relative is that he or she tried to draw us away from Hashem, Who took us out of Egypt. Would it not have been enough had this person tried to draw us away from the Master of the Universe or Hashem Who gave the Torah at Sinai?

R. Samson Raphael Hirsch answers—similar to what we said about a false prophet—that the Exodus was supposed to forever preclude being drawn in by such people. Were someone to suggest that we engage in alien worship, R. Hirsch would say that we shouldn't respond only "that's prohibited," or "Hashem told us not to," but "how could I possibly worship anything other than Hashem, when I *know* Hashem is the sole power in the Universe, since Hashem took us out of Egypt?"

In other words, one more element of the Exodus to be with all of us at all times is its fully and permanently discrediting the possibility of other powers being worthy of worship. That awareness is supposed to be so alive within each of us that we would react with the Torah-mandated hatred and lack of compassion to any person, no matter how close to us, who sought to lead us to worship anything other than Hashem.

It's not an easy standard, nor one we ever hope to put into practice, but I believe it reminds us of just how central the Exodus was in shaping our worldview, how alive it was supposed to be for us, how central to who we are as people and as a people.

Three Surprising Examples
of Jewish Historical Memory

Perhaps our instinct is to think of Egypt and the Exodus as the period of harsh slavery, ending with the Jews walking out. Some might extend it to the Splitting of the Sea, the final act of the Exodus.

Three *mitzvot* take a wider view, seeing events both before and after that as continuingly nationally relevant. They remind us that our national foundational events include more than we tend to realize.

The Practices of the Egyptians

In Lev. 18:3, the Torah introduces a list of prohibited sexual relationships (the עריות, *arayot*) by warning us not to act according to the practices of the land of Egypt, where we lived, and the land of Canaan, where we were being brought. Rashi says the Torah's singling them out as the models we have to avoid tells us their sexual morality was the worst of that era. The verse's stress on "where you resided" in Egypt tells Rashi the Jews lived among the worst of the Egyptians as well.

Of all the places we might have gestated as a nation, Rashi is telling us, Hashem chose the one with the worst sexuality. To me, it reinforces the lesson that sits at the foundation of our nation: Abraham's recognizing the need to reject, forcefully, that which is wrong, even if everyone around you indulges in it, is certain that it is right, reasonable, and respectable. That's easiest (although still not easy) when what's around is *really* wrong; otherwise, we can find ourselves hedging, picking and choosing practices worth adopting.

The Egyptians were so far down the road of perversion that it was supposed to be an easy exercise of our "rejecting what needs rejecting" muscles. That our forefathers didn't succeed in Egypt or Canaan shows how hard it can be, and it reminds us to redouble our own efforts to take on only that which is right and good and to firmly repudiate everything that is wrong and bad, no matter how attractive, and no matter how much those around us—seemingly intelligent, ethical, and well-meaning people—might assert that it's right and good.

The Modernity of the Prohibition

It's particularly apt in our day, because the Rambam (*Sefer ha-Mitzvot* Prohibition 353) accepts *Sifra*'s reading that "the ways of the Egyptians" includes a man marrying a man, a woman marrying a woman, and one woman marrying two men. Remember that Rambam lived in the 1100's, the *Sifra* is Mishnaic, and they were expressing their understanding of what occurred in Egypt, over a thousand years earlier. These versions of sexuality are not some new insight of modern sophisticates, despite their protestations to that effect.

Not only are these forms of sexuality prohibited, they are linked to our experience in Egypt. Part of what we are supposed to remember about our time there is that we were forced to live among those who were שטופי זימה, "soaked in sexual immorality." I think that was supposed to leave us eternally sensitive to such immorality, aware of its dangers and resistant to its temptations, as codified here. But that's not always how it works out.

Excluding the Ammonite and Moabite

Deut. 23:4 tells us that a male Ammonite or Moabite who converts can *never* marry natural-born Jews. Male descendants of this convert will have to marry other converts, in perpetuity, and their decendents can never marry natural-born Jews. This limitation is restricted to this one area: as far as I know, all the special love we owe converts (as we'll see in coming days) applies to these converts as well. It is not that we are unhappy when someone converts; it is that the Torah set up a particular (and challenging) prohibition.

This prohibition is not observed today because we have lost these lineages. Since Talmudic times, we have not known who the real Ammonites, Moabites, or Egyptians are. The prohibitions matter, I think, mostly for what they teach us about our obligatory historical memory.

Because They Didn't Greet You

The Torah gives two reasons Ammonites or Moabites are excluded from marriage: (1) that they didn't greet us with bread and water on our way out of Egypt and (2) they hired Bilam to curse us. Rashi notes the first two words of verse 5, על דבר, which really means "for the fact that," were read hyperliterally as "for the word." The *Sifrei* teaches that this included Bilam's words to the Moabites, advising them to seduce the Jews, exposing them to Hashem's wrath.

The *Kli Yakar* suggests that Rashi was grappling with why the failure to meet us with bread and water would create such a lasting blemish. He thinks Rashi's idea implies that they deliberately refrained from giving us food or drink so as to make us more vulnerable to the blandishments of their women. And it was all Bilam's idea.

One weakness with this theory is that the daily manna was still coming down at that point; perhaps it was the withholding of human connection unless we engaged them sexually—they didn't offer us the succor of bread and water and the accompanying human interaction, in order to make us more vulnerable to the offer of connection.

Part of what we might learn from Ammon and Moab, in the *Kli Yakar*'s eyes, is to avoid the state of weakened resistance to inappropriate blandishments.

We Are Not Blank Slates

Especially if we don't accept the *Kli Yakar*'s answer, his question looms. Why does their failure to offer bread and water deny the Moabite men the right to marry natural born Jewish women *for all time*?

Ramban and *Sefer ha-Chinuch* 561 agree that refusal to provide bread and water reaveals a character flaw, but they identify a different one. Ramban focuses on the lack of gratitude towards the descendants of Abraham, in whose merit Lot and his daughters (the ancestors of Ammon and Moab) were saved. The *Sefer ha-Chinuch* thinks their actions reflect a general lack of kindness.

Your Way Out of Egypt
The *Meshech Chochmah* wonders at the Torah's calling this "on your way out of Egypt," when it actually happened on the verge of entering Israel, forty years later. He answers that as long as we didn't have our own land, we were still "on our way out."

That means the Exodus didn't end the day we got out, or even once we crossed the Sea and never saw the Egyptians again. We were on our way until we arrived.

Were we to know Ammonites and Moabites today, they would be a constant reminder of events long after the Exodus, which the Torah characterizes as on our way out of Egypt. The way they treated us reverberates, affecting their descendants forever.

Keeping Track of the Good As Well
Deut. 23:9 tells us we shouldn't completely reject the Edomite, because he is our brother, nor the Egyptian, because we were

strangers in his land. The third generation of converts from either nation may freely marry other Jews (meaning: the child of a first generation Egyptian convert is a second generation Egyptian, but *his* child, the third generation, is an ordinary Jew. The definition for these purposes follows the father).

It's a strange comment about the Egyptians because, as Rashi and Rosh note, they oppressed us. Rashi focuses on their having killed our sons. What makes that interesting is that Rashi also held that Pharaoh killed Jewish babies only at the time of Moses' birth (to forestall the redeemer from being born), yet he sees that as significant enough that Hashem could have decided to permanently proscribe marrying their converts. Similarly, the Haggadah names their killing our sons as one of the three aspects of our time in Egypt that Hashem "saw" when deciding it was time to redeem us, despite its happening eighty years before the Exodus.

The point that everyone agrees the Torah is making is that when someone provides us a significant benefit, we are *never allowed to forget it.* Since the Egyptians at first took us in and treated us hospitably, we have to hold that good memory, despite their later horrific treatment.

The closest modern parallel might be Germany: for all the atrocities of the Holocaust, our overall picture, if we follow this model, has to include Jewry's having also flourished there for hundreds of years. In many of those years, Germany was the most accepting country in the world for Jews, allowing us the best chance to be full members of society.

Whole Memory, Not Whitewashing Memory

None of this means we should ignore the other parts of the Egyptians' legacy. The passage of three generations before Egyptian converts can marry freely might be to rid themselves of anything Egyptian. The convert is himself an Egyptian; his child is the child of an actual Egyptian. The third generation has no direct connection to being an Egyptian.

An Egyptian who is interested in leaving his clouded legacy can do so—he converts, and waits for descendants free of his former nation. *Then*, the benefit we originally received from Egypt takes effect, telling us we cannot wholly reject these people (as we do the Ammonites, for what would appear a less significant offense).

What makes the Ammonites worse, it would seem, is that no relationship mitigates their evil. In the absence of such a relationship, a relatively little wrong can loom large; in the context of a relationship, even greater wrongs are counterbalanced by other interactions.

How Long Our Memory

We see Egyptians who come to convert through the lens of the good early years along with the bad later ones. Our time in the plains of Moab centuries later is also part of the living past, figuring in our experience of any Ammonite or Moabite we meet; their mistreatment of us, when we were not yet secure or stable, fuels our lasting marital distance from their converts.

Most applicably today, our time *in* Egypt is supposed to be alive for us each time we see certain sexual perversions.

We would have been required to recoil from them even if they were only prohibited. The Torah tells us that, more than that, we should recognize them for what they are—perversions that have been with humanity since the times of the Egyptians. Because our memory is supposed to be that good.

Limiting the Slavery of Jews

The word slavery has very specific connotations in our times, given the horrors that American slave-owners inflicted upon their slaves (and then which other Americans visited upon freed blacks, as Ta-Nehisi Coates has noted in "The Case for Reparations" *The Atlantic* [June 2014]). But the *mitzvot* the Torah sets up around slavery show that the American model of slavery is completely unlike the Biblcal model.

The rules limiting how owners treat their slaves would be sensible and humane without any mention of Egypt; the Torah's connecting three of those to the Exodus adds a dimension that can educate us even when we have none of the permutations of slavery the Torah allowed.

Not the Labor of a Slave

Lev. 25:39-42 starts by referring to your brother becoming poor and being sold to you. As the *Torah Temimah* notes, the Midrash (*Torat Kohanim*) reads that as limiting slavery to the completely impoverished. While we can easily imagine people willing to sign up for six years in a wealthy household, even as servants who couldn't leave, the Torah is letting us know that it is not an acceptable choice for Jews. Servitude happens only out of financial *necessity*, not for convenience.

Second, the *Torat Kohanim* explains that the Torah refers to this person both as "your brother" and as a "slave" in order to lay out the different attitudes of the parties to the relationship. The person sold should think of himself as a slave, beholden to his master, obligated to work as assiduously as he can, as a slave would.

The master, in contrast, should treat and think of the poor person as a brother—one who has fallen on hard times, and whose services have been purchased for these years, but a brother nonetheless. A prominent way the owner shows that attitude is by heeding the Torah's prohibition against forcing the slave to perform עבודת עבד, "the labors of a slave."

Rashi records the definition of the *Torat Kohanim*, which states that the owner cannot assign the slave demeaning labor. His examples were the slave carrying the master's paraphernalia for the bathhouse or tying his shoes. R. Samson Raphael Hirsch adds washing the master's feet, taking off his shoes, supporting the master as he walks, or carrying him on a palanquin, and that the master isn't allowed to lease the slave to others. This last is in contrast to most items we own, which we can choose to rent out.

The problem isn't the effort involved—none of these are backbreaking labor. The *Torah Temimah* points out that Jews may *hire* other Jews to perform these exact services, and that children are allowed to perform these services for parents, as are students for their masters. It is not that these labors are so inherently demeaning that one Jew may never perform them for another. It is the combination of this Jew having been sold (with *halachic* ramifications, such as the master's right to give him a non-Jewish slave as a second wife) along with the demeaning nature of the labor.

Not Selling Them

That sensitivity is also expressed in the Torah's ruling out selling this Jew ממכרת עבד, "the sale of a slave." The *Sifra* (*Behar* 6:1) offers two points. First, it notes that the verse started by saying עבדי הם, "they are My slaves," and My deed came first. A condition of the Exodus was that Jews not be treated as slaves to anyone other than Hashem.

The other meaning the *Sifra* offers, codified by Rambam as Negative Commandment 258, is that these slaves may not be sold on the auction block. Rambam writes that this includes a proscription against standing in the marketplace and calling out the slave's qualifications to attract a crowd of buyers. A Jew may hit a rough enough patch as to have to sell himself into slavery (or indentured servitude), but even then, no one is allowed to compromise his inherent humanity.

A few verses later, the Torah says that a Jew sold to a non-Jew can always be redeemed, by paying the non-Jewish owner the remaining value on the contract. For all that the non-Jew has used the word slavery, it's actually only a long-term contract lasting until the next יובל, *yovel*, the next Jubilee year.

The impossibility of selling a Jew extends to Rav's point in *Bava Kamma* 116b, that we are not allowed to force a Jew to live up to his contract as a day laborer. If the Jew wants to leave in mid-day, and bear the financial consequences, we cannot stop him, because Jews can only be irrevocably indentured to Hashem. Wherever we can enforce it, we have to insist that even a non-Jew allow a Jew early redemption.

Seeing Slavery in a Different Light

Rashi thinks that another part of the Torah's concern with redeeming the enslaved Jew is that his stay in a non-Jewish household endangers his connection to Jewish observance. R. Samson Raphael Hirsch sees it as almost impossible to retain a connection to Jewish observance when in a non-Jewish household.

This is, first, a sobering reminder of how our surroundings impact us. Despite this happening in a Jewish-controlled polity (since we are assuming courts will have the power to make the non-Jewish owner accept the slave's redemption money), the Torah still thinks living in a non-Jewish household will pull the Jew and his family away from their Jewish connection. It also implies that slavery could be welcoming enough that the Jew would want to emulate his master, and that these effects occur so quickly that we must redeem that Jew as soon as possible.

The section closes with verse 55, כי לי בני ישראל עבדים, "for the children of Israel are slaves to Me." Rabbenu Yonah (*Sha'arei Teshuvah* 3:167) thinks this extends to Jewish communal leaders, who must take care not to demand more fear than necessary for their jobs. Submissiveness is how Jews should feel towards Hashem, not humans. While some measure of it is necessary for effective communal leadership, too much is a problem, a hindrance to fulfilling the verse that we are slaves only to Hashem.

The *Aruch ha-Shulchan* (*Orach Chayyim* 473) takes it further, citing this verse to support his claim that the main point of the Haggadah is that we are literal slaves to Hashem. Since Hashem took us away from Pharaoh, to whom we were enslaved, He became our owner. A light slavery, but slavery nonetheless.

Parting Gifts

Deut. 15:12-15 tells slave-owners to gift their departing slaves with, as Rashi notes, items the slave worked with during his time in the master's household that bring ברכה, blessing, such as animals and crops. (Tradition didn't see money itself as something that leads to growth, and did not have to be part of this gift).

The minimum was 30 shekels, the amount owed the owner of a slave gored to death by someone else's ox, as Rambam (*Avadim* 3:14) points out. Rashi cites the Talmudic understanding that the verse expects the owner to add to the minimum, to reflect the level of blessing in the house while the slave was there.

The act of freeing a slave should include setting him up to start a new life, using the tools of blessing the slave had been working with in his or her time with us. That changes the slavery into a sort of extended internship, in which the slave learned skills and abilities and was then given the seed funding, as it were, to build his own successful life afterwards.

None of which, as we've seen before, needs the Exodus in order to make sense. But verse 15 says Hashem is commanding us to do this so that we remember that we were slaves in Egypt, from where Hashem redeemed us. Rashi explains that we would be imitating Hashem, who ensured we left Egypt and the Sea with much wealth.

Three *mitzvot* about slavery remind us of how to treat others; more than that, they remind us that Hashem took us out of Egypt in a way that both set us up for a successful financial future and converted us into permanent servants, an allegiance that, at a minimum, we cannot allow to be superseded by anything else.

Treating Converts Well and Carefully

The Torah warns us many times about the sensitivity necessary to deal with the stranger/convert. Exod. 22:20 and Lev. 19:33, two central texts, warn us not להונות, *le-honot*, the stranger and also not ללחוץ, *lilchotz*, him or her. The Talmudic assumption is that the words indicate verbal and monetary abuse respectively.

There are many good reasons to treat a convert well, but the Torah connects it to the fact that we were strangers in Egypt. That might seem obvious—having been in a similar situation, our knowledge of how it feels should lead us to do better—but commentators differ on what it is about Egypt that should shape our reaction to converts. That in turn affects our understanding of how our time in Egypt is supposed to resonate for us today.

The Pot Calling the Kettle

The *Mechilta de-Rabbi Yishmael Mishpatim* (*Masechta de-Nezikin* 18) quotes R. Natan as focusing on the tone-deafness of mocking a stranger, since we bear whatever flaw we might think to point out in them, having been strangers in Egypt. Rashi records that statement in Exod. 22:20.

Neither R. Natan nor Rashi explain why Egypt counts as a blemish. One answer might be that we tend to point out how strangers stand out, since they are still unfamiliar with the modes of behavior customary in their new place. Jews who do that to others are allowing themselves to forget when they were oppressed by their host culture. Since we were strangers in our first moments as a people, struggling to keep up with a culture we didn't know (and never got in full step with, refusing to adopt their names, language, or clothes), we should know better than to treat that as a flaw in others.

Hashem brought us to Egypt intentionally—a way to sensitize us as a people to how it feels to be out of step, to have compassion for those struggling with the understandable uncertainty of inhabiting a new culture.

Part of the memory of Egypt, in this version, is to remember when we were unsure of ourselves, to ensure we never become too certain of ourselves. That piece of it can apply even when there is no stranger or convert around.

It Hits Them Differently, and They Might Chuck It

That same *Mechilta* mentions the view of R. Eliezer, that the Torah is reminding us that our comments to a stranger/convert impact him or her differently than other Jews. His phrase is שסורו רע; one way to read that phrase is as Rashi does to *Horayot* 13a, that converts are more prone to sin. Perhaps their newness to the religion, society, and culture gives them an incomplete hold on values that seem second nature to us. If they become frustrated by how they're being treated, one reaction might be to rebel and violate the Torah; we are obligated to make sure we are not the cause of the convert regressing in spiritual development.

The *Sefer ha-Chinuch* 63 offers what I see as the simpler reading, that they might decide to abandon Judaism entirely. Either way, we are being told to remember when we had a tenuous connection to a way of life, how easily we could shuck it off. Realizing that strangers and converts are at that delicate stage should impel us to avoid doing anything to jeopardize their station in life.

It Hurts Them More

Exod. 23:9 reminds us that we know the *soul* of the stranger, which Rashi understands as a reference to the stranger's feeling slights more intensely than others treated the same way. (Tosafot, *Kiddushin* 70b, thinks such people are so sensitive that it's almost impossible to never hurt them.) What fuels that feeling?

The *Sefer ha-Chinuch* 63 ascribes their sensitivity to their relative defenselessness, their lack of protectors or friends and relatives who see it as their privilege and responsibility to stand up for them when attacked. Even if they develop some of that, they feel like they have less of it than natural-born Jews.

Entrenched Insecurity, According to R. Yitzchak Arama

The *Akedat Yitzchak,* the philosophical/homiletical Torah commentary of R. Yitzchak Arama (15th century Spain), thinks feelings of insecurity can linger even once a convert becomes integrated fully in Jewish society and develops a support system. After all, seventy family members went to Egypt, with much wealth, and still, over time, the Egyptians enslaved us. Because we were not natives.

R. Arama also reminds us that the stranger/convert may interpret any verbal and financial attacks as a function of status, even if it isn't. Should a Jew bring an ordinary lawsuit against the convert, the convert might assume (wrongly) that it's only being done because of that outsider status.

We should know to be sensitive to that sense of isolation, because we felt that way in Egypt.

Ramban and R. Bachya: Egypt as a Window on Hashem

Ramban focuses on the defenselessness of the stranger, taking it in a more Hashem-centered direction. We are only tempted to take advantage of the stranger since he or she has no protectors, but our experience in Egypt should remind us that Hashem is their protector, as Hashem was ours. For Ramban, Egypt might also have taught us sensitivity and humility, but it was primarily about the picture of a Universe whose Master has a particular interest in, and concern for, the helpless and the weak.

R. Bachya says Egypt should show us that treating the stranger/convert with care is an instance of emulating Hashem, shaping our characters to be more like Hashem, as it were.

The *Minchat Chinuch*: How Far Does It Go?

The *Minchat Chinuch* wonders whether these laws apply only to an observant convert. The Biblical prohibition against verbally abusing an ordinary Jew explicitly refers to עמיתו, "his fellow," which teaches the Gemara that this is limited to Jews who strive to fulfill the Torah. The Torah places no such parameter on the obligation to avoid mistreating a stranger or convert; it seems logical to extend it, but the Torah does not, and it might be different.

The *Minchat Chinuch* also wonders whether a descendant of converts—someone who may be a tenth-generation Jew, but all of whose ancestors were converts—would still qualify for these rules (such as, perhaps, a member of a community that converted and married only within the subcommunity, generation after generation). This person is not defenseless, and has a well-established communal base, friends, and family.

In that sense, such a person isn't a stranger. On the other hand, we do consider that person a convert for other purposes (such a person could not be appointed king, for example, because a king has to have some natural Jewish lineage). For all that they have *some* family structure and support, their keeping so strictly to themselves perhaps also indicates that they still feel like outsiders.

Besides, the Torah treats all of our time in Egypt as if we were strangers, not just the first generation. So too with converts, it seems to me; as long as they haven't intermarried with ordinary Jews, whatever the reason, they are separate, and we have to worry that they feel that separateness, and we would therefore be obligated to treat them with the Torah-mandated care for their feelings and sensitivities.

Loving the Convert

The Torah also obligates us to love the convert, as in Lev. 19:34 and Deut. 10:19, again explicitly connecting it to our having been strangers in Egypt. Rashi repeats his comment about not pointing out in others flaws we ourselves bear, seeing this as the flip side of the prohibition against mistreating them. In Mitzvah 431, the *Sefer ha-Chinuch* also defines the obligation and gives examples that are the obverse of the prohibition against mistreating them. Sometimes love is the other side of mistreatment, with no middle ground.

Rambam (*Sefer ha-Mitzvot*, Positive Commandment 207) says Hashem added a commandment to love the convert because the convert came to join our Torah; he points to Midrashim that compare this love to the love we are supposed to express for Hashem. For Rambam, we cannot mistreat the convert because we remember Egypt; we have to love the convert because the convert has chosen to join those who worship the one true God.

R. Bachya notes that the Torah precedes the command to love the convert with a verse that speaks of Hashem's loving him or her. If so, we emulate Hashem by acting this way (similar to what he said about why we have to avoid oppressing the convert).

Neither Rambam nor R. Bachya explains how this obligation is connected to our having been strangers in Egypt.

R. Samson Raphael Hirsch offers an answer that they might have ratified. He says that Egypt should have taught us that the failure to welcome and treat a stranger with basic rights mutates into the hatred and mistreatment we eventually experienced at Egyptian hands. Welcoming with love might be the only antidote to sliding into hatred and abuse.

It seems to me also plausible that, for Rambam, memories of Egypt would include how hard we found it to accept Hashem—our doubts about Moses, the distressingly large numbers of Jews who didn't make it out, our difficulties accepting a new discipline. Remembering those struggles, we would look at those who voluntarily undertook them with admiring, loving eyes.

Important as these *mitzvot* are on their own, they are here another example of how what we went through in Egypt stays alive throughout our lives, in this instance showing up every time we encounter someone new to Judaism or to our land, a convert or a stranger. It's right to treat them well; for us, it's supposed to be even more so because we remember Egypt.

Weights and Measures, Interest, Gifts to the Poor, and Bugs: A Grab-Bag of Egypt-Related *Mitzvot*

As we near the end of our time together, we will take up *mitzvot* the Torah connects to Egypt with the least clear link. We'll start with financial ones.

Weights of Judgment, Judgment of Weights

Lev. 19:35 warns against perverting justice in weights and measures, to have accurate scales, and reminds us that Hashem Who took us out of Egypt, commands this. The smaller problem is that the Torah had warned us about perverting justice, using much the same phrasing, eighteen verses earlier. Rashi articulates the implication, that the Torah repeats itself to make clear that weighing or measuring accurately, in a private transaction, is akin to judging a court case properly.

Judges are punished for failing at their job, and we would likewise be pubished if we used improper weights and measurements. Just as *Sifra* (*Kedoshim* 2:4) tells us that perversions of justice defile the Land, desecrate the Name, banish the Divine Presence, and lead to losses in war and to exile—so do improper weights and measurements. Rashi adds that those who cheat with measurements, like corrupt judges, make themselves disgusting and an abomination, cut off from closeness with Hashem.

Why Egypt?

All societies have laws about keeping accurate weights and measures. Why connect it to the Exodus? R. Ya'akov Tzvi Mecklenburg in *Ha-Ketav ve-ha-Kabbalah* points out that we can make the mistake of thinking we follow rational obligations *because* of their underlying rationale. For Jews, he says, that would be worshipping our rationality instead of Hashem. To emphasize that Hashem's command must be the bottom line of *all* observance, Hashem mentions the Exodus.

Rashi captures much of that with three words, על מנת כן, "on this condition," Hashem took us out. Hashem took us out of Egypt and thus obligated us to observe *each* commandment. Weights and measures is almost a coincidental example; each time we keep the Torah, regardless of whether the Torah expressly related it to Egypt, we fulfill an agreement we made in Egypt. Weights and measures is one occasion the Torah paused to remind us of that original promise.

A More Specific Link

Rashi also references *Bava Metzia* 61b, where Rava asks why the Torah mentions Egypt specifically regarding *tzitzit*, the prohibition on eating bugs, charging interest (both of which we'll see), and weights and measures. Rava's answer, each time, is a variant of the idea that Hashem, Who differentiated the first-born from not (Egyptian promiscuity meant no one in Egypt really knew who was a first-born), would differentiate those who think they can hide their transgressions of these commandments.

People would dip their weights in salt, which either made them heavier (Rashba) or lighter (Rashi). Either way, it is a means of defrauding the other person without the victim realizing it; the verse reminds us that Hashem sees and knows all (Meiri expands this to any area where we can cheat with impunity).

The *Shulchan Aruch* (*Choshen Mishpat* 231) says cheating in this way constitutes a denial of the Exodus. The Exodus demonstrated Hashem's awareness of all that happens, even in our most private places and moments. Hidden cheating repudiates what we were supposed to know ever since we left Egypt, that we are never truly alone, private, or hidden.

Interest

Lev. 25:38 similarly closes the prohibition against taking interest from fellow Jews by reminding us of Hashem's having taken us out of Egypt. Rava explains that just as Hashem differentiated between first-born and not, Hashem will differentiate those lending a non-Jew's money from those who pretend they are, to cover up their usury.

We need not discuss the technicalities of when a loan is considered to have originated with a non-Jew, such that one is allowed to charge interest—there is voluminous literature on the subject—to see the same message here as in weights and measures: we have to be aware of Hashem, especially at those moments when no one else will notice. The experience in Egypt is what should ensure our awareness of that.

R. Hirsch reads both of these verses as Hashem warning us that our right to belong to a society depends on submitting ourselves to Hashem's discipline. Refraining from charging interest announces our recognition that our money and our society comes from Hashem.

Along those lines, R. Yosi in *Bava Metzia* 71a notes that people who write out loan agreements incorporating impermissible interest summon witnesses, a scribe, quill, and ink to announce their denial of Hashem. They would physically fight someone who called them an evildoer, but here make a public spectacle of their evil actions.

Rambam (*Malveh ve-Loveh* 4:7) phrases R. Yosi's statement as their having denied the *Exodus from Egypt*, not Hashem in general. The *Shulchan Aruch* (*Yoreh Deah* 160:2) includes both, it is as if the person denied the Exodus *and* the God of Israel.

Harvest Gifts for the Poor

Moving to one more mitzvah with a large financial component, Deut. 24:22 closes the list of obligations we bear to the poor during the harvest by saying that we have to remember we were slaves in Egypt, which is why Hashem is commanding us to leave part of our crops unharvested, as well as leaving behind any parts of those fields, orchards, or vineyards that we forgot to harvest.

Here too, the obligation to set up a social safety net and, perhaps, help include the poor and dispossessed in the national excitement over the harvest seems a worthy set of obligations, without any reference to the Exodus. Yet the Torah wants us to give these gifts with the memory of our slavery in mind.

The *Kli Yakar* reads this obligation as aimed at those who claim they cannot give because they have to build an inheritance for their children. Financial prudence, these people said, prevented them from giving charity. What it really shows, the *Kli Yakar* says, is that these people failed to absorb central lessons of the Exodus, including the lesson that all wealth comes from Hashem. A lesson we should know, since we were once slaves in Egypt and are now pursuing our own estate planning.

Allowing the poor to glean *and* giving them money we might have stashed for our heirs are, for the *Kli Yakar*, two ways to affirm our belief that Hashem controls and confers wealth. Money isn't only money; it's a sign of our awareness of Hashem's involvement in our financial lives. And we were taught that awareness on our way out of Egypt.

Not Eating Bugs and the Exodus

Lev. 11:44 tells us to make ourselves קדוש, *kadosh*, for Hashem is *kadosh*, and we shouldn't make our souls טמא, *tamei*, with any crawling insects. The next verse has Hashem declaring Himself as the One Who took you (us) out of Egypt to be your (our) Hashem, and you (we) should therefore be *kadosh*.

146

Kadosh and *tamei* are commonly translated along the lines of "sanctified" or "holy" and "ritually impure." That those terms are used about eating bugs will expand our definition. As a first step, the Torah seems to be saying they sully our souls, negating or impairing our sanctity. We are required to avoid that because it hinders our striving to be as קדוש as Hashem, Who took us out of Egypt, precisely to be our God.

Three commentators shed light on the ambiguities in that statement.

Sforno: Eating the Wrong
Foods Distances Us From Hashem

Sforno understands Hashem to say that one goal of the Exodus was for us to need fewer or no intermediaries in our contact with Hashem. Refining our characters and intellects is the way to do that, and eating bugs damages that refinement.

He makes two assumptions, first that our moral and intellectual level determines how directly we can connect with Hashem. The more developed we are in those realms, the more sanctified we are, and therefore the closer to Hashem. Second, of course, Sforno is saying that eating bugs gets in the way of that closeness.

In that reading, we call Hashem *kadosh* only in the sense that improving ourselves in these ways brings us closer to Hashem. The references to Egypt and the Exodus are to remind us that that closeness was a central purpose of those events, so we should do all we can to foster that relationship. Bugs are a good example, but just an example.

R. Hirsch: Careful Eating as
a Path to One Kind of Sanctity

R. Samson Raphael Hirsch sees קדושה as a ladder; by sanctifying our physical senses, suppressing our baser desires, we ascend to truer freedom and ethics. The call for *kedushah* here (and with prohibited foods generally) is to remind us that checking our physical appetites is a first and continuing step of that process.

Even should we achieve full (or some level of) such sanctity, R. Hirsch says, we must always guard our physical selves, so that we do not backslide and re-defile our souls, negating the hard work we had put in to achieve that *kedushah*.

According to R. Hirsch, the Torah makes this connection in regards to insects, because eating them is emblematic of yielding to our senses; controlling that is the first necessary step to growth.

Being "Brought Up" or "Brought Out"

To understand how R. Moshe Feinstein understood the prohibition of eating bugs, we have to review a conversation between R. Chanina of Sura of the Euphrates and Ravina reported in *Bava Metzia* 61b, where the former asks why the Torah mentioned leaving Egypt in connection to bugs.

Ravina says, a line we've seen before, that just as Hashem differentiated first-born from other children in Egypt, Hashem will know and punish those who mix permitted and prohibited species of fish.

R. Chanina persists. His question was more specific, wondering why the Torah here said, "Who brought you *up out of* [המעלה אתכם] Egypt," whereas in the similar cases of *tzitzit* and usury, the phrase was, "Who took you out of [המוציא אתכם] Egypt."

R. Moshe Feinstein, in *Iggerot Moshe Orach Chayyim* 1:15, reads that Gemara as telling us that not only were we taken out in the merit of our performing all the *mitzvot*, but that any one of them would have been sufficient to justify our leaving. He bases that conclusion on the Torah's seeing the avoidance of bugs as sufficient to justify the Exodus, despite their being disgusting. Other *mitzvot*, which we obey solely because of Hashem's command, all the more so.

How Proper Memory of the Exodus
Would Shape Us Differently Than Now
With only one more mitzvah to review, today's *mitzvot* showed how broadly the Torah included remembrances of the Exodus. Our finances, charitable giving, and diet are all linked back to Egypt.

Granting commentarial differences, we saw, several times, the suggestion that the Torah was reminding us that all the commandments we observe are grounded in Egypt, that the entirety of our Jewish lives is a function and extension of Hashem having taken us out of Egypt.

First Born, First Fruits, and Concluding Thoughts

First-borns matter. Rambam lists eight Biblical commandments relating to first-born animals or people, and Ramban
adds another, meaning that a percent and a half of all Biblical
commandments show us how to deal properly with first-
borns. Studying the significance the Torah gives these issues,
why it sees them as so important, will remind us of another
oft-forgotten life lesson of the Exodus.

Stress on the Killing of the First-Born

Exod. 13:14 tells us that when our children ask why we
dedicate our first-born animals to Hashem and redeem our
first-born children, we should tell them that the Egyptians
resisted Hashem's command and Hashem killed their first-
born. Twice in Numbers (3:13 and 8:17), Hashem justifies
the exchange of first-born for Levites by noting that Hashem
had "acquired" them on the day the Egyptian first-born were
killed.

That Egypt focus is, as we've seen with other *mitzvot*,
not the only way we could have found a rationale for these
obligations. The *Sefer ha-Chinuch*, for example, explains that

by dedicating the first products of our endeavors—human, animal, or plant—we actively recognize that all that we have comes from Hashem.

Three unusual aspects of the commandments regarding first-born point the way to an explanation of the Exodus focus. Rambam (Positive Commandment 79) notes that the *Sifrei* includes only animals born in Israel. This is derived from the fact that the Torah incorporates tithes and first-born in one verse (Deut. 14:23)—just as tithes only apply in the land of Israel, so did the first-born.

A second issue is that the Gemara derives the prohibitions against working or shearing all sanctified animals from the Torah's declaration about first-born animals (Deut. 15:19), as Rambam notes in *Sefer ha-Mitzvot* (Negative 113-114). It's surprising that first-born became a paradigm for all sanctified animals, since other rules of the first-born are so different, such as that they can be eaten in all of Jerusalem for two days and a night.

A final feature that will take us towards an explanation is Ramban's view that there is a positive obligation to eat first-born animals in Jerusalem (the more basic message of Deut. 14:23). Rambam had ruled against eating them elsewhere (Negative Commandment 144), but Ramban thought he wrongly omitted an active obligation to eat *maaser sheni* (the second tithe) and first-born animals in Jerusalem. Ramban stresses the Torah's saying that part of the point was that we should learn to fear Hashem.

Do *Kohanim* Need to Learn to Fear Hashem?

It is obvious that Jerusalem is where a Jew would be most likely to encounter the Torah's influence. The *Sefer ha-Chinuch* 360 says that a Jew who comes to Jerusalem to fulfill the commandments of *maaser sheni* will also take those positive influences back home.

First-born animals, though, are eaten by priests. It's less obvious why the Torah would insert occasions to draw the *kohanim* to Jerusalem. Shouldn't they be there anyway, as part of their required Temple service?

To me, the answer starts with a Mishnah (*Zevachim* 14:4), that prior to the establishment of the *Mishkan* (Yerushalmi *Megillah* 1:11, quoted by the *Torah Temimah* to Num. 8:17, who connects it to the sin of the Golden Calf), the first-born functioned as priests. Had that continued, the functionaries of the Temple wouldn't have been a separate tribe, different from ordinary Jews. They would have been the first-born of every family.

Jews would have gone to the *Beit ha-Mikdash* and seen sons, brothers, cousins, and other friends and family members. Much like *Sefer ha-Chinuch*'s idea that even one family member bringing tithes to Jerusalem would affect the whole family, staffing the *Beit ha-Mikdash* with first-born would have spread the experience and messages emanating from Jerusalem more organically throughout the people.

That might explain why the plague of the first-born was the breaking point. If the Egyptians, too, took special pride in their first-born, Hashem's striking them was a blow that went beyond the actual loss. When the Egyptian first-born died, that even threatened all of the Egyptians because the first-born *were* the nation, in their minds. In a sense, their society was being destroyed, because they had so much invested in the first-born.

If so, the *Chinuch's* reason for redeeming the first-born and first fruits might connect to Egypt as well. By dedicating our successful first yields to Hashem, we remember that such firsts were also Egypt's pride and joy. Since Torah society orbits around Israel (as we'll see more sharply when we get to בכורים, first fruits), only there does first-born's role as symbols of the whole society become relevant.

All this also shows why the Torah would use first-born to set up a paradigm for how to treat all sanctified animals. Dedicating our first-born to Hashem was a crucial part of becoming Hashem's people, in contrast to the Egyptians' pride in their first-born, which fortified them in remaining a corrupted people; as a first step in our service to God, it makes sense to become the standard for other acts of service of God.

First Fruits

First fruits share three qualities with the first-born animals: they are presented at the Temple, they can come only from the Land of Israel, and they are thematically connected to the Exodus from Egypt. In the case of first fruits, each of these is intensified. It's not enough to bring the first fruits; we make a parade of it (see Mishnah *Bikkurim* 3:2-6). These offerings come only from species that the Torah identifies as the pride of the Land of Israel, and as we offer them, we recite a summary of the Exodus story (*Arami Oved Avi*), a recapitulation that captures the events so well, we use the same passage on Seder night as the backbone of the Haggadah.

Rambam (*Guide for the Perplexed* 3:39) wonders why we would mention the troubles of Egypt in the context of thanking Hashem for the bounty we received in Israel. He notes that wealth can foster arrogance and complacency. Wealth can instill a sense that all is well, that we need not change in any way, and require the assistance of nobody, even Hashem.

The Torah helps us combat that sentiment by commanding us to remind ourselves of when we were impoverished and oppressed. That will reduce our complacency—if we keep in mind how miserable things were in Egypt, we will be more likely to remember that things can deteriorate. In addition, instilling in ourselves the firm memory that the good came from Hashem will hinder our falling into the trap of thinking we developed it ourselves.

Living the Dream

Despite Rambam's logic, his rationale does not explain why we had to reach back to Jacob and Egypt. What would have been lacking had we thanked Hashem, acknowledging aloud that all our wealth comes from Hashem, without the Egypt story? Is that the only way to instill humility?

I think there's another element, shown in two verses we don't include on Seder night. When the person bringing his first fruits gives the basket to the priest, he must say, "I declare today to Hashem that I have come to the Land that He promised to our forefathers" (Deut. 26:3). Why must this declaration be made?

Someone bringing first fruits also says more about Egypt than we say Seder night. The extra verse that says that Hashem brought us to this Land, flowing in milk and honey. Why make that part of the first fruit ceremony?

The first fruits, the Torah seems to indicate, are the proof that all the promises to the Patriarchs have come true. Even though we went down to Egypt, and endured a prolonged slavery, Hashem took us out, as promised, brought us to the Land, as promised, and here we are, living the dream, doing what Hashem set up as the model and the ideal.

Each year, as we live the dream, we remind ourselves that we're in the right place, doing the right things, and how wonderful that is.

First-born, first fruits, firsts in general can endanger or enrich us spiritually. They can lure us into feeling overly comfortable, overly certain the future will go as well as the recent past. Or, as the Torah helps us see, remembering the Egyptians' misuse of their first-born, and that the produce of Israel is the proof of Hashem's involvement, can let us react to our first-born in a way that improves our relationship with Hashem, instead of damaging it.

Taking Transformation Forward

As Pesach winds down, let's pause to reflect, to see the forest I hope we've built out of our daily trees.

The central lesson I hope we have learned is that the Torah and *halachah* codified many of our reactions to the Exodus more explicitly and specifically than we sometimes stop to realize. Many Jews put sincere and strenuous effort into their observance, even their Pesach observance, while seeming to miss much of what I believe we have seen are clear and explicit messages and lessons of our having left Egypt.

We started with the story as told in the book of Exodus, since the brief treatments in the Haggadah itself can lead us to forget the richness of how tradition saw the events. We sought a path towards a fuller Seder, particularly in fulfilling one *halachic* requirement of Seder night—seeing ourselves as if we left Egypt. To capture that moment, we tried to put ourselves back there, reviewing choice-points of the main characters in the story.

Watching them fail and succeed helped us, I hope, see ourselves doing the same or different, bringing to life some of what it would have been like to go through it, how it would have felt to be eating that first Paschal sacrifice, loins girded for an imminent journey back to a land we had only heard about from our fathers and grandfathers, had never ourselves seen.

A successful Seder is a worthy goal, but the Exodus' impact on our spiritual personae should not end on the Seder night. We analyzed how the commandments, individually and collectively, closely tied to the themes of the Exodus from Egypt, and how the frequency of those commandments enforces the Exodus in our hearts and on our lips, reminding us of fundamental principles about how we are supposed to see the world.

We are the people who left Egypt, not under the influence of social, cultural, or political forces, but because the Creator and Master of the Universe בכבודו ובעצמו, in all His glory, as it were, came to take us out. Based on our experience of leaving Egypt, we should confidently assert for all time that the world is created, not the happenstance result of laws of Nature; that its Creator is and always has been involved in events in this world; that the Creator is omnipotent, able to shape human events however and whenever He so chooses; and that this Creator has chosen and commanded the Jewish people to represent these truths throughout human history.

Our observance of Pesach, of Seder night, of telling the Exodus story, are not complete unless and until we allow the truth of these statements to permeate our lives, as the Torah and *halachah* modeled for us. Daily recitations, periodic observances, but even more so our ordinary conduct teach us to be that people, to have our thoughts, words, and actions reflect this awareness, shape who we are, in all ways.

I hope the twenty one days we've spent together have been of service in that regard, have helped each of us come closer to living that reality, to converting belief statements into truth statements, accurate summaries of how we understand how the world works. And to live our lives in more and better service of our Creator, the God Who took us out of Egypt.

PART II

My Father's Seder, Foundation of My Faith

12:45 a.m.: *Afikoman*

April 20, 1970—I was almost five and a half years old; the "and a half" mattered back then. We were living in California. The Seder was in the dining room, to the left of the entrance area from the front. Through that dining room, you came to the breakfast nook connected to the kitchen. The side door of that kitchen was where we would come back in to the house after the San Fernando earthquake on February 9 of the next year.

But that was still to come, and wasn't nearly as bad (for us) as it might have been. I slept through it, my mother got a good scare grabbing the baby (also not around at that Seder), and we lost one crystal decoration off the chandelier over the dining room table, around which we had been seated that Passover.

A table that had come with us from Washington, D.C., would stay with us for our three years in a third-floor walkup in Brookline, our two years in a two-family in Flatbush, and then join us in the move to the house my parents would live in for the twelve years until my father's sudden passing at fifty, my age as I write these words.

I moved over those years as well, from his left to his right and from having a whole side of the table to myself to sharing with siblings eating into the exclusivity my older sister and I had had. But that Passover night in Los Angeles, as I itched for us to get to the *afikoman*, the last piece of matzah eaten at the Seder, I had the left side to myself.

My father was at the head, his back to the ceiling-high wooden cases filled with books. Those cases also accompanied us on our moves, until my mother gave them to me (I quickly destroyed them through misuse, but that's a different story). They loomed over me for decades beyond my childhood, a symbolic repository of the knowledge I needed to become a confident adult, like my father. Although he once disagreed, telling me that what I saw as maturity and certainty was an act he felt he had to put on for us kids.

That Pesach night, the bookcases had a simpler role; they were the limit of how far my father was willing to look for his missing *afikoman*. His seat allowed him to look directly across at my mother and, beyond her, out the windows onto the street. However, he always insisted on covering the windows with shades, his discomfort with outsiders looking in outweighing any pleasure of looking out.

Passover night, his resistance to outsiders paid dividends I would only see later. Since leaving his house, I have been at many Seders (*Sedarim*, for the nitpicking Hebrew-speakers among us, which usually includes me) that include guests, and I recognize and appreciate the value in sharing the night, having been both beneficiary and benefactor of such hospitality.

My father's Seder was strictly family and, except for occasional years at his mother's, or with his brother and my mother's sister (who are husband and wife), nuclear family at that. It meant the Seder ran exactly as he wanted, except for nudges by my mother to move it along.

Dictatorships often oppress, but the benevolent rule of my father's Seder gave his children an experience I have never been able to recreate or match. I hope the reasons for that will become clear as I invite you to join in my reconstruction of those nights.

I have to be the one to extend the invitation because my father is no longer with us, so you have no hope of attending the Seder he ran. I choose to invite you because in six or fewer remarkable hours, twice a year, my father packed in a lifetime's worth of content, emotional attachment (to God, to Judaism, and to each other), and religious belief. To experience my father's Seder was to come away changed, broadened, enriched.

The other participant in Seder 1970 was my older sister, the Seder professional, until that night the one who had always taken the *afikoman*, generously allowing me to hang on her coattails as she chose where to hide it.

Among the many ways to involve the children in the *afikoman*, our family's way was that, at the same point every year, my father would use the restroom, leaving the *afikoman* unguarded. That was the cue for his pilfering children to take action. When it came time to eat the *afikoman*, he would make a tremendous show of looking for the missing *matzah*, hamming it up in a way he never did the rest of the year, finally resigning himself to buying it back from his poorly parented offspring.

At five and a half, I was ready to do the deed on my own. I had apprenticed a few years, there were two nights of Passover, two of us—my other sister was two months away—and I wanted my solo shot. All went smoothly at the moment of theft, my father leaving to use the bathroom, me, probably with elephantine grace and noise, bringing the goods to their hiding place in my room, down the long hall just behind my seat.

Cut to 12:45. All right, I admit I have no idea whether it was really 12:45; in all likelihood, it was not that late, because my father worked to make a Seder his children were interested in joining. In later years, when my sister and I (and younger siblings) had more to say, we ran longer, and often did not manage to get to the *afikoman* even by 12:45. That night, I assume it was somewhat earlier.

But it was certainly late, later than I generally stayed up, late enough that, even with my pre-Passover nap and the adrenaline rush that kept me going, most years, until the end of the last song (often 1 or 2 a.m.), I was probably tired.

My father brought the curtain up on the high theater of searching for his *afikoman*. In the first act, he reached into the pillows on which he leaned throughout the Seder. Moving casually at first, not expecting any problems, since he had inserted *matzah* only hours earlier. As it failed to turn up, a first hint of puzzlement flashed across his face. Befuddlement turned into concern as he checked the floor, beginning to confront the fact that his *afikoman* had been stolen, not just fallen from his pillow.

In the second act, after a narrated intermission wondering what could have happened, he took a look around the room, back through the bookcases, as if the *afikoman* might have abrogated the laws of physics and migrated there, his patter taking on a tone of growing urgency.

All received by my sister and myself with the appropriate hilarity. We knew he knew who had stolen the *afikoman*; we knew he was putting on this show for *us*, that the histrionics were entirely for our benefit, one more way to make the Seder fun, to do his best to ensure we would carry this with us every day and year of our lives.

Adding to the comedy, although I did not then know it, was the drama's complete superfluity, as a relative with a slightly crueler sense of humor made clear to me only a couple of years later. That was the year we drove from Boston, where my father had moved his stay-at-home-wife and three children to attend law school, to Washington, where my grandmother and assorted other relatives lived.

It offered more men, meaning my sister and I could steal our way to a present each night. This relative was otherwise one of the bright spots of my childhood, a man who did not yet have children of his own, whose home I loved visiting, not least because the ice cream flowed more freely than in my parents' house.

But he was armed with the dangerous knowledge that Jewish law has no requirement that the *matzah* eaten for *afikoman* be the *matzah* put away at the beginning of the Seder. And he decided to have a little fun. He had his wife get my seven-year-old attention, long before *afikoman* time, had me watch as he noticed that his *afikoman* was missing, and then simply replaced the missing *matzah* with a fresh one from the box.

I'm pretty sure he later came across with a gift, but the romance was gone, at least for that ritual with that relative.

None of those dark clouds were on the horizon in Los Angeles in 1970, the excitement building as my father became increasingly concerned, then agitated. I was at the edge of my seat, ready to begin the bargaining that would end in the promise of a gift. What gift I wanted has been lost in the family legend of that night, which came to a head in the next moment.

Because my father brought out his absolutely best material, capping it with, "Well, I guess we'll have to call the police to help us find out who stole our *afikoman*."

That was it. I was out of my chair and down the hall, ready to give the damn *matzah* back to the crazy man who had replaced my father. As I write these words, the tears that came to that five-year-old's eyes come again, that moment of fear still fresh and alive.

But here's the thing. The person most upset about the outcome of that little play was my father, who had said those words only in the hopes of eliciting more of the merry laughs he had been seeing until then. And as I ran down the hall, it was him racing after me to bring me back, calm me down, assure me he had been joking, and promise me (I assume) a better present than I otherwise could ever have dreamed.

My father's Seder, a legend in the minds of each of his children, certainly in my own, perhaps embellished in our memories by having lost him suddenly and identifiably earlier than we had any reason to expect. It started with the *afikoman*, exciting for the way my father handled it, and, of course, the prizes that came out of it.

Those prizes were special for reasons other than their extravagance, since they weren't. The years in Boston were ones of financial discomfort, although not poverty. We never worried about where the next meal would come from or if we would have clothing, thank God, but it was a time when luxuries, like extra toys or vacations, were out of the question. My father's decision to leave computers and switch to law had many positive aspects, but they put a financial crimp in our lives that would only recede when I finished high school.

Before those more comfortable times, there was the year of the $5 limit on our *afikoman* presents, which even then was not a lot of money. My mother, whose heroic handling of many of the circumstances of our lives deserves a discussion of its own, found me a baseball glove that came in under the limit. It was probably worth only what we paid, but it did me fine for years.

Presents were also fun because my dad helped build them and then played them. I suspect the board game *Landslide*, a fixture of Sabbath afternoons in Boston and still the foundation of my understanding of the electoral map of the US, was an *afikoman* present; if it wasn't it could have been, and my father spent many more hours with me and my sister over *Landslide* and other games than I could have had any right to expect.

I offer these memories as my enticement to come see the rest of his Seder, one of the best ways I know to bring the Exodus alive, to make it real for us, in our days.

A disclaimer on times and characters. I lead off each segment of this recollection with a part of the Haggadah, and a time when my father would have gotten there. These are both approximate and composite; the family Seder was not so regimented that we arrived at the same point at the same time each year (although my mother trusted our pacing enough that she always put the *matzah* balls in the soup at the same point in the Haggadah).

Some years we went later. Mostly, we tried to finish the story and eat the *matzah* between 10:30 and 11, two to three hours after we started. That depended on whether we had changed the clock, whether it was the first or second night of the holiday, and so on. I include times as a way to convey the flow of the night, not out of any claim to exactness.

I have told the story, mostly, as if there were only two characters, my father and me. Not that I was the most important person at his Seder, but because each of his children was important to him, on Seder night particularly. I have made it about me and him, with the occasional intrusion, because I remember our interactions more vividly than the rest, and because it was those interactions that made the night, for me, *My Father's Seder, Foundation of My Faith.*

8:00 p.m.: Hopening the Haggadah: The Order of the Night and *Kiddush*

That is no misprint in the title, it is my word for how opening the Haggadah felt each year. Hoping that that year's Seder would be as exciting, enjoyable, and as late (important for bragging rights) as last year's. Or more so. "Hopening" also prepares you for the punnish humor my father brought to the evening and to his life.

We never started at eight, even when Passover began before the clock changed. On the second night, we had no chance of starting that early, because we couldn't prepare until the first day was over. The men and boys could only undertake their tasks, minor as they were compared to my mother's, when we got home from evening services.

I well remember the sense of the ticking clock as I scouted the house for pillows whose owners would not complain at having their sleep aids inundated with crumbs of *matzah* and grape juice stains from the four cups we'd be ingesting.

My father used two pillows on his armchair. I moved from a symbolic one behind me to a separate chair with three stacked on it and, eventually, to an armchair of my own. It has never been comfortable, but tradition was and is tradition.

It's an odd way to characterize my father, an instinctive iconoclast, equal-opportunity slaughterer of sacred cows, in

Judaism, general morality, and society at large. In religion, he balanced that attitude with a fundamental commitment to tradition.

He could have found traditional support for relinquishing leaning. That is how in the sixteenth century the Rema, R. Moshe Isserles, justified women not leaning. While the Talmud obligated only "important" women in leaning, medieval Ashkenazic Jewry saw their women as important in that *halachic* sense for other purposes. Still, the women did not lean.

The Rema, whose glosses to R. Joseph Caro's *Shulchan Aruch* (*Code of Jewish Law*) became the central codification of Ashkenazic practice, explained (*Orach Chayyim* 472:4) that women rely on the twelfth-century German Ravyah, R. Eliezer ben (son of) Joel ha-Levi, who held that reclining is no longer necessary (for anyone), as it has ceased to serve as a sign of freedom. Exactly the kind of idea I would have expected my father to embrace, respecting a tradition's original reason and noting when it no longer applied.

On Seder night, the weight of custom ruled, leaving me to scrounge for pillows, a task that became more difficult as my younger brothers reached ages where they wanted their own as well—if my father and mother had the armchairs, three boys looking for three each got to be a lot of pillows.

Finally, we'd be ready. My father would stand at the head of the table in his white *kittel*, the plain robe he wore Seder night, Rosh Hashanah and Yom Kippur, and then to his final rest on a mountaintop outside Jerusalem.

On the latter three occasions, the robe marks the limitations of life. Rosh Hashanah and Yom Kippur are days of judgment, the wearing of the *kittel* during services a reminder of the balance in which our lives hang. The year God's judgment decreed his life would end on Chanukah, the *kittel* was his shroud. Seder night, it marks the head of the Seder as royalty, an aspect of the freedom God gave us this night.

After chanting the order of the Seder for the benefit of the youngest, most families went straight to *Kiddush*, the blessing to note and acknowledge the special qualities of Sabbaths and holidays. But my father would pause to remind us that the first page of old German *haggadot* had a picture of a rabbit hunt, and challenge us to remember why.

To understand the humor behind that, we need to detour to a brief Talmudic discussion. When the first night of a holiday occurs Saturday night, the opening to the festival meal has to combine the ceremonies of *Kiddush*, welcoming the day, with *Havdalah*, bidding farewell to Shabbat. There were many opinions about how to order the five blessings being folded into one recitation.

The mathematician in my father would have noted that there are 120 possible ways to combine them, but fewer than ten are mentioned in the Talmud, in the form of an acronym for the order of the blessings. In the Talmudic system of classification, Y stood for *yayin*, the blessing over wine, K for *Kiddush*, the one announcing a special day, N for *ner*, candle, the blessing on fire recited at the close of Shabbat, H for

Havdalah, celebrating God's separating the sacred from the mundane, and Z for *zeman*, time, thanking God for keeping us alive to reach this occasion.

Jewish law ratified the order YKNHZ (pronounced *yaknehaz*, with both *a*'s said as *ah*). To get from there to the picture in German *haggadot*, we need most of the smidgen of German he taught me. I say that with regret, since I never managed to absorb the language. As a child, I wanted to learn it because relatives spoke it to each other—my grandmother and her sister, God rest their souls, would start jokes in English, slip into German without realizing, and then be puzzled when no one laughed at the punchline.

I think I got as far as that a spoon was a *löffel*. Years later, I needed to pass language exams for my Ph.D. The French went fine, but the German? By the skin of my advisor's very generous teeth, is all I can say.

The three words from Seder night I did remember. A rabbit, or hare, is a *hase*; "hunt" is *Jagd* (I thank Google Translate for refreshing my memory), so that the German for "hunt the hare" would be *Jagd den hase*, close enough to YKNHZ, *yaknehaz*, to serve as a mnemonic.

Until I finally remembered it on my own, my father would bring it up year after year, the same twinkle in his eye, his joy undiminished by the repetition. His love of puns was lifelong and longstanding. My uncle used to tell us how his much older brother would torture him with the claim that Wyatt Earp's real name was Earp Longhedrickson. My uncle knew it wasn't true, but couldn't shake my father's certainty.

He would challenge him that the world knows him as Wyatt Earp, but my father would reply that that was because of an incident when Earp was once in a saloon. An outlaw took a shot at him, but missed, knocking off his hat.

Longhedrickson turned around, said, "Why at Earp?" and the name stuck.

That fascination with language and its possibilities passed to me, fed my choice of a dissertation that focused on what counts as a plausible meaning. How did commentators know which interpretations were too far outside the pale to accept? How did they know, in the various contexts in which it came up, the difference between YKNHZ and *Jagd den hase*, between real readings and playful ones?

Part of that was also about rules of a genre, and that, too, figured in my father's sense of humor. His two favorite jokes during my childhood derived whatever small humor they had from how they violated convention.

The first, "What weighs 800 pounds, is yellow, and sings? Two 400-pound canaries," was opaque to me until, on the "umpteenth" (one of his favorite words) time he'd told it, I confessed I didn't get it. That was when he shared that canaries weigh five pounds or less, so the idea of a 400-pounder did not even make it to the level of ridiculous. Then I got it. Sort of.

He would also periodically take me through the following conversation: "What is red, hangs on a wall, and hums? A herring. But a herring isn't red!? So you paint it red. But a herring doesn't hang on a wall!? So you hang it on a wall. But a herring doesn't hum? So it doesn't hum, so sue me!"

To see him wearing the *kittel* because that's what tradition said, even as he celebrated the puns of *Jagd den hase* and the rules-bending humor of his favorite jokes, typifies the balance he strove to strike, that night and in general. Rules were to be followed, but not mindlessly nor in a way that robbed the underlying fun. The start, middle, and end of Seder night left a good taste, however many times in between or in the run-up I ran afoul of his rules and his temper.

We would recite *Kiddush* together, as opposed to the rest of the year, when my father recited it and we answered, "Amen." This would spark the first of several examples of a routine I never quite understood. I'd ask why we were acting differently. Or maybe one of the other kids did; I don't want to imply I was the only active participant, because that's far from the truth. On the other hand, those who write the history shape it.

The parental answer, from both ends of the table, was, "So you should ask." For a long time that sounded reasonable, until I realized that piling up meaningless changes to elicit questions with no answers is self-defeating, since it might teach kids—me—not to bother asking.

It's like the joke my father told me (or maybe I told him): A man's walking with his son, and the son says, "Why is the sky blue?" The father thinks and thinks, and says, "I don't know, son, that's a good question." They walk a little further, and the boy asks why the grass is green, and gets, after another pause, the same answer. They walk further, and the boy asks why stop signs are red, to once again be told that while it was a good question, the father did not know.

The fourth time, the boy opens his mouth, then stops and says, "Oh, never mind." His father says, "No, ask, ask, how will you ever learn if you don't ask?"

Luckily for those of us at my father's Seder, more than a few of the questions *did* have answers, often multiple ones.

8:10: Doing What We Want or What We're Told: Drinking the Grape Juice, *Urchatz* and *Karpas*

After *Kiddush,* we drank the first cup. I never cultivated or developed a taste for wine, so until adulthood I resisted the reality that Jewish law preferred wine for Seder night, barring some kind of physical intolerance. Until I made the switch, the four cups were an unaccustomed pleasure, a burst of sugar back when I could still absorb that much without ill effects.

The leaning detracted, because spilling earned a paternal glare for clumsiness. Other than that, the cups went down smoothly, certainly the first. That first cup had much work to do, because I would have had little to eat for most of the day. Any non-Passover products, bread, cereal, and the like, were prohibited from somewhere in the 9:30-10:30 range that morning. At the same time, custom ruled out *matzah*-based products, since that would detract from the experience of fulfilling the commandment. I could eat all the fruit I wanted, but that got old fast for a five-and-a-half-year old.

By family tradition, my mother made salami and fried potato slices for lunch, one of the few times a year I ate potatoes that weren't officially French fries. After—and I could eat only so much salami and potatoes—there was a distinct lack of options, meaning that first cup had to make up for earlier in the day and tide me over for the next two hours.

Not a child of much self-control, my instinct would have been to down it. My father, however, was fond of noting the Talmud's declaration that gluttons drained it in a single gulp, while sipping was a sign of prissiness. At four, I hadn't had a choice—I couldn't finish a cup in fewer than several drinks anyway. As I progressed to where I could knock it off at once, my father's words turned what I had thought would be a marker of prodigious ability into an unwanted sign of weakness.

Two drinks a cup it was, and then the long wait until the *matzah* came around.

I don't want to exaggerate. A little before we got to the *matzah*, there would be a few drops of grape juice to suck off our fingers, the remnant of our expression of sympathy for the Egyptians' suffering during the ten plagues. But that would do little to assuage the hunger and thirst I had built up by then; it was basically a *Kiddush*-to-*matzah* marathon.

What's that, you might say, there is the *karpas*, the appetizer we eat soon after *Kiddush*, a sign of wealth and freedom, since only rich people ate appetizers.

Well. Yes. Hmm.

Before we talk about *karpas*, we have to watch my father go to the kitchen to wash his hands, without a blessing. This triply contrasted with the rest of the year, when we only washed for bread, everyone who was eating washed, and we made a blessing as we wiped our hands.

Here at least, questions had answers. Why no blessing? I would later learn that the custom of washing originally included any food susceptible to impurity, laws more observed in Temple times than today. Hands are impurity-prone, and washing them was a way to avoid transmitting that to any foods being handled.

With the destruction of the Temple, the Sages instituted hand-washing as an act of memory. *Karpas*, produce dipped in salt water, fits that criterion.

By that logic, we should wash our hands before handling all such foods, including wet produce, but, other than for bread, washing has long fallen into desuetude. Passover night, the washing before *karpas* was an expression of the freedom to observe the law maximally, to keep all its dictates to their highest form and extent.

Then why only the father? Some families do have all the attendees wash; our custom was that the head of the household's washing demonstrated our sense of freedom. In fact, some families brought the water to the head of the Seder for further emphasis of his royal standing that night.

He would go, wash, come back, and hand out those pieces of *karpas*, which theoretically contributed to staving off hunger during the long recounting of the Exodus story to come.

But there were a few problems. First, my family ate radishes. Others, like my in-laws, ate potatoes. Since I don't like potatoes either, that wasn't much of an upgrade, but I could see how it would be somewhat filling. Us? Radishes.

I did not like radishes, and not in the *Green Eggs and Ham* sense. I knew what radishes tasted like, I ate them at the Seder every year, and I knew I didn't like them (still don't, in fact), which is no knock on the many good people who earn their living in planting, harvesting, and bringing radishes to market. More power to them, and may the Good Lord bless them and keep them... far away from me and my plate.

To make it worse, the living embodiment of another old Jewish joke, not only didn't I like them, the portions were small. This was intentional, part of how my father's family custom resolved two longstanding questions of Jewish law.

Later in the Seder, we were going to eat *maror*, the bitter herb. Ingesting items that aren't food doesn't require a blessing, such as medicine. Jewish law wasn't clear on the blessing status of *maror*, food that's eaten precisely because it's bitter.

The other problem was the blessing after eating. If we ate a certain amount of *karpas*, we would seem to have to recite a blessing, thanking God for the food.

Our solution to these problems—there are others—was to keep the bitter herb in mind as we recited the blessing over *karpas*. "Keeping in mind" at my father's Seder meant that he would ask us each year what we were supposed to remember as we made this blessing, as if we hadn't learned it the previous year, and the one before that, and the one before that.

That was one side of his Seder in a nutshell: exact repetition, articulating all the reasons and rationales for what we were doing, until we could run one of our own, in our sleep (as I sometimes do, now that I am older and more tired).

Embarking on telling our Exodus story, which would involve many mixed messages, I already had a living paradox of my own—an act, supposedly for the purpose of emphasizing a sense of freedom, that instead obligated me, by force of tradition, to do something I didn't enjoy all that much.

And in a self-contradictory way, we dipped this sign of wealth, this symbol of freedom, in salt water, in memory of the bondage. I wouldn't say I saw the irony, but I did notice the gap between the words we were saying and the reality I was feeling.

It was an early and implicit lesson in what R. Abraham Joshua Heschel and others called the difference between "freedom from" and "freedom to." "Freedom from" loosens bonds and leaves us to drift or stride wherever we wish, with no guarantee or confidence we will use that freedom wisely. "Freedom to" shows the road to live up to God's standards. Superficially less free, it guides us to a life that will be, in total, freer and truer to who we are and need to be.

I never came to appreciate *karpas*, and my children follow their mother's practice of eating potatoes, but past the *karpas*, we were going to get to the telling of the Exodus story. That I *did* enjoy, and from a very young age. It was and is, for me, the greatest example of balancing freeform storytelling with rigidly disciplined order to produce a masterpiece, year after year.

8:15: *Mah Nishtanah*, Do It Right

Yes, the drama around *karpas* took no more than five minutes. There was the handing it around on a spoon, the brief reminder to mentally apply this blessing to the bitter herb, and then the eating. Occasionally, someone had an idea about how and why we eat the *karpas*, but there were few enough of those to take much time.

After *karpas*, we (often I) poured the second cup. The freedom of Passover night militates for someone other than the head of the table to dispense the drinks (free men have servers—in my father's case, me). It wasn't difficult, except that my father insisted on filling his cup to the brim, a traditional sign that God keeps our cups full with bounty.

"Filled to the brim" did not and could not mean overflowing, not in my father's house. Years later, I became friends with a man who *insisted* on overflowing his cup, because his tradition was to show that God's bounty was overflowing; my years of struggling to reach the brim without going over had me recoiling and wincing at the ease with which this man broke those bounds.

It was also harder back then, because the gallon jugs were glass. The beginning of the pour was easy, you put the spout of the bottle to the cup and let fly. As the grape juice rose to the top, timing was all. Stay in pouring position too long, it spilled over; pull back too soon, there would be clear daylight between the juice line and top of the glass, and I'd have to top it off.

Only now, I'd have to maneuver that heavy bottle to pour just a bit more. Going from largely full to all full without going over was, to me, a challenge of almost Olympic proportions. But my grape juice skills came along at a reasonable pace, because practice does make better (although never perfect, not in pouring, not in life, not for me), and by 8:15 or 8:30 (depending when we actually started), we were likely ready for מה נשתנה, the Four Questions.

As at so many Seders, the youngest stood to ask. Youngest, in my father's home, was a charmed time of life, when the child had to go to sleep at a certain time and couldn't throw food, but other than that, until four or five or six (it got longer with each child), he didn't believe they were ready for real discipline. So their older siblings (me!) had to cope with each prince or princess until their time came to be ushered into the ranks of civilized society.

Seder night, in one sense, was the same. As the whole family cleaned the apartment or house, to be sure there were no overlooked crumbs of bread, crackers, or the like, this youngest's only job would be to ask the Questions. We would arrive at the anticipated moment, and the youngest would stand, ready to wow the table. The table, in turn, looked on expectantly and smilingly, sure to be blown away by his or her adorable rendition.

Mostly, that's what happened. The child sang, we all oohed and aahed, and the Seder continued, except for a frequent hiccup that marks a way to understand my father and his Seder. This youngest often was not yet literate, was singing as he or she had been taught. And they were often taught wrong, by my father's lights.

See, the first of the four questions deals with eating *matzah* as opposed to leavened bread, and there, the contrast is simple: on all other nights, we eat both, as we wish, while on this night, it's *all matzah*, because God prohibited any leaven for that night and the rest of Pesach.

The next question notes that this night we eat *maror*, a bitter herb. But many *haggadot*—more important, many elementary school teachers—phrased the question as a repeat of the first, teaching, "On all other nights, we eat other vegetables, on this night, *kullo maror*, all *maror*."

Uh-oh. It's *not* all *maror*, as my father would point out. A valid point, except that when you're lower single digit years old and have learned a song (by heart, because you can't read, so it's not like you could remind yourself to skip that word *kullo*, "all"), it's not so easy to change.

Which I have to assume my father knew and understood, but right was right and wrong was wrong. By the time my brothers were doing it, my older sister and I were explaining in advance, the reasoning beyond them at that age. They forgot and said it anyway, but at least weren't completely bewildered when my father corrected them, as my younger sister had been.

In fairness to my father, his insistence relaxed with each child, balanced by his interest in a fun Seder for the little 'uns. The edge of anger at our imperfections, which my older sister and I knew so well, dulled over the years.

We two older ones used to half-complain as we saw him treat the sibs so gently. We would mock the easier parents they had, in both discipline and finances. My father would always say, "Yes, but you got us (he and my mother) younger."

When events went as they did, he won that argument for all time. We older two had him until we had reached some meaningful form of adulthood, whereas the younger ones lost him in their childhood or adolescence. I'm pretty sure he meant it more in terms of energy levels, his interest in playing with us—certainly none of my younger siblings coaxed as many hours of cards or chess out of him as I did.

You might think my father's insistence on getting the Questions right was nitpicking, but you'd be wrong, because he didn't nitpick. One of his favorite quotes was Ralph Waldo Emerson's "a foolish consistency is the hobgoblin of little minds." He especially enjoyed noting that many people misquote it as "consistency is the hobgoblin of little minds." He was all for consistency, but not foolish consistency.

It wasn't a foolish consistency that had him correcting whether we said "all *maror*" or not. It was part of conveying the value of getting it right. Being corrected, being reminded I had not yet done as well as I could, was a consistent part of my childhood and, from the vantage point of aduthood, a positive and constructive one.

There were at least two ways in which he had given me a too-rare gift, and which, as he mellowed, he backed off on giving my younger siblings. First, repeated self-examination and self-correction is a deeply Jewish ethos. Repentance, in Jewish thought, involves the readiness, nay, the certainty, that none of us is perfect, with the corollary that each of us has room to improve.

To find that room, we must identify current lacks; the less defensive we are, the more open we are to seeing those problems, the more likely we are to find our way to repentance, to an improved relationship with the God whose salvation we celebrate Seder night.

Learning that mistakes aren't the end of the world, and that the one who points them out to you is often doing you a favor, also prepared me to more than once learn from brilliant teachers whom others avoided for being prickly or difficult.

To me, their concern with preparation, with doing a job well and properly, with nailing down truth to the extent possible, were not only not intimidating, they were like being home. I profited more from those classrooms than I can express, and my father's training readied me, intellectually and emotionally.

One of those teachers once corrected me on my pronunciation of a word in Old French. A Talmudic commentary we were using inserted an Old French term to explain a Talmudic one. As part of our preparation, we were expected to look up the term, since the exact definition could affect the point being made. I was called to read the text in question, and misread the word (I don't speak Old French).

When I asked him why I should care, he thought I was questioning the value of knowing what the word meant, and launched into an explanation of how we could not be sure we understood the comment correctly unless we knew what the word meant. I explained that I was asking why I had to know how to *pronounce* the word.

He shrugged and said, as my father might have, "If you're going to do something, you should do it right."

My father's ultimate triumph was the extent to which I am able to confront my own failings and try, yet again, to improve (whether or not I succeed), as well as the years I benefited from teachers I might have abandoned, had my father not taught me the value and the pleasure of getting it right.

I am richer for it.

8:45: Cultural Openness Without Enslavement: *Avadim Hayinu*, We Were Slaves

No, it didn't take half an hour for *Mah Nishtanah*. Although, the year I was fifteen, when I did it in French, my fourth-grade sister in Yiddish, and my five-year-old brother in Hebrew, it might have taken fifteen minutes.

I padded because I've probably been optimistic with time. I've skipped, for example, the short ideas we used to share about הא לחמא עניא, the paragraph before מה נשתנה that declares the *matzah* the anchor of our Seder. I've also ignored removing and returning the Seder plate ("Why? So you could ask!"), so by now we were probably already well behind schedule, some quarters of the table lobbying to move faster.

Easier urged than accomplished. עבדים היינו, *Avadim Hayinu* ("we were slaves to Pharaoh in Egypt") was no simple matter—there was agreeing on a tune and then singing it, which our musical failings made harder than you'd think. But the centerpiece of our experience of this paragraph was my father's insight into the Haggadah's noting that if God had not taken us out, הרי אנו ובנינו ובני בנינו משועבדים היינו לפרעה במצרים, "behold we, our children, our children's children, would be enslaved to Pharaoh in Egypt."

Cue the actor in my father, puzzled confusion on his face. "Really? We would be slaves to Pharaoh if God hadn't taken us out?"

I'd look in the *Haggadah*. "Yeah, that's what it says, we, our children, our children's children, would be slaves to Pharaoh in Egypt."

His long stare, reminding me to *think*. "Do you *see* any slaves in the world?"

Had I known then what I do now, considering the smartaleck I was, I probably would have made a comment about human trafficking. Instead, I gave a dumb shake of the head, unable to explain what the בעל ההגדה, the compiler of the Haggadah—to whom we always addressed our questions about the text, a presence as real at my father's Seder as any of the attendees—intended by these words.

Being confounded by simple questions was a regular feature of my childhood. Friday nights, for years, he and I would replay a conversation, for reasons I could never quite grasp. I'd go to school all week, listen well enough that my teachers had no complaints. My father would work all week, so hard that, for many of those years, I saw him only for brief breakfast conversations from Sunday to Friday afternoon.

Come Friday night, with the leisure enforced on him by God's commanding the Sabbath, he would turn to his eldest son, one of the sources of pride and joy in his life. Interested in the education he was slaving to afford, dear old Dad would say, "So, Gidon, what did you learn in school this week?"

Complete blank, on my face and in my mind, each time. To this day, if you ask me what I'm working on, I go blank.

Seder night I was helped by our all using the same text, so my failure was only in finding an answer, not the ground for the conversation. Having the text in front of me didn't tell me what the Haggadah meant by saying we would all be slaves to Pharaoh if God hadn't taken us out.

My father would give an answer, but one lesson had already been taught. Texts make sense; when they didn't, it was my job, as reader, to ferret out what was missing. That was why, when I *did* remember something I had learned in school, he would probe my understanding, quickly stumping me with what seemed, to him, an obvious question. When I didn't know, he would ask, amazed, "Well, then, why didn't you ask?"

To say I hadn't thought of that question was implicitly unacceptable; my job as a student (and, eventually, teacher) was to think through what I had learned, to be able to answer others' questions and to be able to phrase myself well enough that it was all understood. We spent many long and frustrating occasions with him insisting I repeat my presentation of an idea until it flowed smoothly and logically. Before that, he'd refuse to understand, because the way I'd said it didn't make sense, and he would not let me get away with that.

When I complained, he'd say, "Do you know the definition of a mathematical proof?" "No." "An argument that convinces another mathematician." Or, "if you can't explain it to someone else, you don't really understand it yourself."

All true, but not a big help to a child whom the author of the Haggadah had stuck with his claim that we would still be slaves to Pharaoh in Egypt, when the American slaves had been freed more than a hundred years before.

It took a while, but I got it. For a few years, I'd forget the question from one Seder to the next. Then for a Seder or two I'd remember there was a question, but not what it was. Then I'd remember the question but not the answer. Only then, after enough repetitions, was the question and answer rooted in my being.

He taught us that we mistranslate משועבדים לפרעה as "we would be *slaves* to Pharaoh," when in fact (get it right!) the Hebrew word means we would be *enslaved*. "Enslaved" can be slavery, but it can also be a deep enough sense of indebtedness, financial or emotional. Had we left because Pharaoh freed us, our gratitude would shape our world; we would retain connections to Egypt by virtue of the great gift their king had given us.

More, had they freed us, we would never have had the distance to see the corruption of their culture and worldview, how it conflicted with the ideas and ideals God was about to teach us. God taking us out Himself, as it were, freed us of that.

I always liked the textual insight; it took longer to grasp the message it sent about the culture around us. I grew up in a home that willingly partook of Western culture—we watched TV, read most kinds of books, went to many movies. There were books and shows my father ruled out as inappropriate, but I grew up in an America where my home values felt like they fit right in with the "outside world."

But I also always knew we were different, so that this Haggadah comment wasn't at odds with the rest of the year. There was our familial connection to Israel, where we almost moved in the early 1970's. Not as a rejection of the US, but as an expression of another commitment. It didn't pan out, but the memory remained and remains.

Our move from Brookline to Flatbush, when I was almost ten, introduced me to the "right-wing" world, which rejected more of American culture. Down the block from our ground-floor rental of a two-family lived two men who had gone to Chaim Berlin with my father, but looked much more right wing. One was visibly Hasidic (to my fifth-grade eyes, that marked him as the most right wing possible) and the other was *yeshivish*, ordinary level right-wing. You could see it in the hat he wore, his children's sidelocks, but also their allowed forms of leisure, which excluded TV.

At some point, I turned to my father and said, "When did you change so much from your *yeshiva* days?"

"I didn't change; *they* did."

In his memory, their *yeshiva* believed in going to college at night, and grappled with living real lives in the modern world in a way that the people down the block from me did not seem to be doing.

When he told us about Hashem freeing us of Pharaoh and his whole culture, it wasn't out of a hope that we would sequester ourselves. It was as a reminder that we immerse in Jewish culture, and critically engage other cultures. Some of which were so corrupt as to need to be rejected completely and totally. Like Egyptian culture.

We were slaves to Pharaoh in Egypt, and God took us out, freeing us from lingering obligations to them or their culture. As free men, I learned at my father's Seder, we are able and expected to engage all cultures we encounter, but critically. To see where they could enrich us without drawing us in so fully that we lost sight of our Jewish commitments, lost touch with our need to stay faithful to that which God had told us. To adopt those aspects of their lives that would improve our service to the Master of the Universe, enhance our relationship with God. Only those.

And reject those parts that didn't, freed of them by the Exodus.

9:00: *Ma'aseh, Harei Ani,* Inclusivism, Old and New, Rational and Supernatural

Nine p.m., and we were finally underway in earnest. *Avadim Hayinu* ended by telling us that we had to recite the story at length, regardless of how wise, smart, and knowledgeable we might be, and the more, the better. Music to the ears of a boy intent on *shul*-yard bragging rights.

The Haggadah's preference that we tell the story at length took us to an example, five great rabbis who spent the entire night recounting the Exodus, becoming so caught up that their students had to summon them to recite the morning Shema. We place the incident here, my father would point out, as a practical example of what "at length" could and should mean. These rabbis, leaders of their generation, were certainly well familiar with the story, could have rationalized telling it briefly and returning to other important matters, yet they threw themselves fully into it.

Just as they did, so did my father. Despite his having a well-formed, insightful, and coherent reading of the Haggadah of his own, he welcomed and incorporated new ones that came along. While he generally preferred straightforward readings of texts, he came to favor an allegorical explanation of this paragraph I learned in elementary school, making sure someone at the Seder said it each year.

R. Akiva is known for his support of the Bar Kochba rebellion (among his many contributions to Jewish history), and the story is set in Benei Berak, his hometown. One of my teachers taught us that it was incongruous to imagine that the students had to remind their masters of the technical fact that they needed to say the morning Shema. Granting that they had become engrossed, and had no windows, is it feasible that they lost track of time to that extent?!

This teacher suggested instead that the location is included in the story to imply that R. Akiva set the agenda for that year's Seder. The deliberations were not about the original Exodus, but whether the time had come for another one, a rebellion against the Roman oppressors. They argued the whole night, the old guard for appeasement and accommodation, the new guard—including R. Akiva—pushing rebellion. When the students came, they weren't speaking of the morning Shema literally, they were saying it was the dawn of a new day, a new era of freedom for the Jewish people to worship God.

A more straightforward answer to the original question would be that the ideal time for Shema is before sunrise, and the students were helping their teachers remember to say it in that time frame. But this reading offered an answer close to my father's heart, for its cleverness and content. The idea that we could convert a humdrum Pesach night tale to a consideration of when it was time to overthrow the existing order thrilled him, as did (I think) the students' taking it upon themselves to inform the masters of their view.

From then on, someone recited it, annually, at his Seder, modeling his hope that our Seder nights would grow into two-way streets, we absorbing what he gave, reciprocating with what he had not yet encountered.

One of the other attendees at that Seder in Benei Berak was R. Elazar b. Azaryah, who then tells of his long-running failure to convince the other scholars of his generation that the Exodus story had to be mentioned nightly as well as daily. Although he was "like" seventy years old, he had never managed to prove that the Biblical obligation of daily mentions of the Exodus included one at night.

Ben Zoma found the desired proof, based on a reading of the verse, למען תזכור יום צאתך מארץ מצרים כל ימי חייך, "so that you shall remember the day you left the land of Egypt *all* the days of your life." His derivation followed a common rabbinic practice, insisting that a superfluous word—in this case, כל, "all"—added something we might have missed. Days of our lives would mean once a day; *all* the days, Ben Zoma said, taught us to mention the Exodus at night as well.

My father would wonder why the Haggadah included the story at all—in his way of making clear that he had an answer he wanted to share, but wanted you to be clear on the fact that you hadn't anticipated his question, let alone intuited the answer—since it analyzes the obligation to speak of the Exodus the rest of the year, not Seder night.

Ben Zoma also didn't quite prove his point, since the Sages thought that the word *all* informs us that the obligation of speaking of the Exodus daily will continue after the

Messiah comes. We might have thought (as Jeremiah 16:14-15 and 23:7-8 seem to say) the return to Israel and rebuilding of the Temple would overshadow it.

What did Ben Zoma's insight, and R. Elazar b. Azaryah's introduction of it, have to do with our Seder? My father's answer came in three stages. First, he quoted his father, quoting *his* father, and so on back into the haze of generations, that the debate hinges on how we understand the word כל, "all." According to Ben Zoma, it means "all of," the entirety of an item or day, not just one part. The Sages read "all" to mean "each and every," telling us to include days we might have thought exempt.

The focus on text and close reading, of which this was but one example, eventually gave me a topic for a Ph.D. dissertation, but also got in the way of his and my attempts to study Torah together. We would start, every once in a while, because fathers and sons *should* learn Torah together, and then get stuck, because he wouldn't let me get away without knowing the basic text. I remember my struggles with the word זרעיך, "your descendants," in *Bereshit,* which I for some reason could not remember. Or why the first Mishnah in *Bava Metzia* asks litigants to swear they own no less than half the item when they're actually claiming the whole of it.

Each time we came to it, he wouldn't move on until I had mastered the text itself. Same with his discussion of R. Elazar b. Azaryah and Ben Zoma; the first step had to be understanding the debate in its textual sense.

Then we would go broader. One of us—usually the youngest, who had most recently learned the famous story—

would explain that when the Sages offered the vacant position of head of the Sanhedrin to the eighteen-year-old R. Elazar b. Azaryah, he had hesitated, fearing that his older colleagues would not respect a man of his youth. Overnight, the Talmud tells us, God put eighteen streaks of gray in his beard, so he could comfortably accept the position.

My father would always make sure we noticed that in R. Elazar b. Azaryah's time, looking *older* was the way to secure respect. Letting the youngest tell that story both brought that child into the conversation and opened the way to his next problem, why it was relevant *here*. Unless we're to believe that R. Elazar b. Azaryah said that each time he spoke, the implication is that that incident in his life is relevant to the discussion he is launching.

The simplest reading is that R. Elazar b. Azaryah was noting that one might have thought his having been the recipient of a public miracle would itself convince his colleagues to listen to him about the times to say Shema. That doesn't quite work, since then he should say it each time he introduces an *halachic* discussion he did not win, not just here.

The family tradition suggested that he was noting the contrasting messages of two parts to the Exodus story. At night, Hashem killed the Egyptian first-born, an event that proved His involvement and removed all hope of being able to resist. The slaves' leaving Egypt the next morning was miraculous, their having secured their release against the will of the most powerful nation on Earth (at the time). But it worked within the laws of nature.

How we time our mentions of the Exodus, my father would say, depends on our attitude towards miracles. The daytime part, the leaving, is an example of Hashem's usual bounty, goodness bestowed upon us within the framework of the natural.

When events occasionally "force" Hashem, as it were, to perform a miracle that abrogates nature—such as graying someone's beard overnight—our reaction has some complexities to it. We might focus on the recipient's having been worthy of this; R. Elazar b. Azaryah might look at his beard and enjoy knowing that Hashem valued his becoming head of the academy enough to affect events directly.

On the other hand—a whole worldview comes with this "other hand"—Hashem made a world that operates regularly, with rhythms we identify as nature. When needed, Hashem can and does step in, even openly, such as in killing Egypt's first-born. But is that good, to be celebrated, or proof the world had gone so far wrong as to need extraordinary measures?

That, my father suggested, was the question about the night-time mention of the Exodus, with ramifications for our Seder night telling as well. If we mention the Exodus at night, we are saying those miracles, too, deserve retelling. If not, it implies that we should spend our Seder on the more natural parts of the events, as signaled by only mentioning the daytime leaving the rest of the year.

It would also affect R. Elazar b. Azaryah personally, shaping his narrative of his life-shaping miracle as a reason either for unmitigated joy or an example of where the world wasn't up to progressing naturally. For my family, it was a reminder that as rationalistic as we generally were, we had to always be open to the possibility of obvious and open miracles, had to recognize some miracles as historical facts, to be celebrated, since we do mention the Exodus at night.

Which we were working to relive that night, each in our own way, as the four sons showed us.

9:15: The Four Sons, Engaged Parenting

One of the more popular and famous passages in the *Haggadah*, there was little special in how we kids, like children the world over, pointed at each other as the wicked or simple son, at ourselves as the wise one. We did not stop to notice that the Haggadah makes the goal wisdom, not intelligence, since it deems wise the child who asks the right question, wanting to know all the (in his phrase) "testimonies, statutes, and laws the Lord our God commanded us."

My father expanded the Haggadah's parenting lessons by calling our attention to its use of the same verse for both the wicked child and the one who does not know how to ask. In the Haggadah's presentation, we tell them בעבור זה עשה ה׳ לי בצאתי ממצרים, "because of this that we do (the Paschal sacrifice and its attendant practices), Hashem took me out of Egypt."

When the Haggadah read that as directed to the wicked child, it made a point of noting the verse's implied bite, the stress that Hashem took *me*, the parent, out of Egypt, because I would do this service. Asking "what is all this work to you?" excluded that child from feeling obligated by this service. Redemption would have passed him by.

All well and good, my father would say, but then why does

the שאינו יודע לשאול, the child who does not know how to ask, receive the same answer, with the same implied rebuke?

I should interject the background that at my father's Seder, we assumed this child was too young to know how to ask.

Over the years, as we accumulated *haggadot*, with varied illustrations of the four children, we saw that some artists thought all the children were the same age. In those, the simple child and the one who did not know how to ask were mentally limited or didn't care enough, respectively. That view could see something lacking in the שאינו יודע לשאול, could see an implication in the Haggadah that the child is apparently so far removed from the religion that the ceremony is one confusing jumble. That's the road to becoming wicked.

With many more Jews in that position today than at any other time in history, those illustrations raise complex questions about how we view Jews disconnected from and lacking interest in tradition. That was not the child we dealt with at my father's Seder, so we can leave that for another time.

My father's explanation, delivered yearly with the knowing tone of one who has a secret his children will only fully appreciate when they have children of their own, was that the sting was directed back at the wicked child. Sometimes, he would say, a child is *so wicked* that he or she would not tolerate the insinuation that he or she would have been left behind.

With that avenue of communication blocked, the *Baal Haggadah* was telling us, the parent should turn to the שאינו יודע לשאול, the child too young to ask and therefore too young to pick up on the allusion, and say the crucial verse. The wicked son would not be able to take umbrage (a favorite word of my father's), since it was not directed at him.

From what I've seen in the intervening years, my father's idea doesn't quite work in practice, since difficult children find the same offense in indirect rebuke as direct. But it was an example of his interest and effort to be the most effective parent he could, a rich mix of discipline, joyful fun, and everything in between.

For the discipline, suffice it to say that he found the ways to effectively convey the necessity of certain parts of life. On the other hand, it was my father who did much of the work in helping me learn to read when I wanted to; who before my Sabbath afternoon nap told me stories from Tanach that were so exciting I can still remember the wonder they instilled; who would spend hours playing cards on long Shabbat afternoons when friends, TV, or other forms of entertainment were unavailable or had been used up; who filled hours-long family car rides with games of Ghost and Geography when I no longer had the patience to read; who, during his early years as a lawyer, when there was no spare money for entertainment, when he was billing insane hours, entered the firm lottery for tickets to sporting events, to take me, despite his having long lost interest in sports.

I asked him once about that. How could he not love sports, all the trivia, all the interesting tidbits about players and their accomplishments? He smiled, said he too had followed it avidly when he was younger, but it had come to seem insignificant as he got older. One of those parental statements that give them the last laugh, the child in question following his father's footsteps depite his oath never to become like that.

Those games, back then, were highlights not to be missed. We once arrived at a Knicks game as they introduced the players. The law firm's seats were, obviously, far better than any we would have bought on our own. Just to get to them was memorable, since we came out of a tunnel right behind the Knicks bench.

The usher took our tickets to lead us to our places, and the announcer called Glenn Gondrezick, who was perhaps three feet away from me at that moment. I can't remember a single other Knick who played that night, I have no idea who they played against, the score, or who won, but I was *right there* when Gondo was announced, a memory that will likely leave me only when dementia sets in.

There was baseball and hockey, too. I don't remember much about those games other than the quality of the seats, I don't remember actual words in Ghost he or I won or lost on, I don't—mostly—remember the places in Geography. I remember that my father, a very busy man, with plenty of reading to entertain him for the rest of his life, was always interested and excited to play with me, to help me have a good time as well, for the enjoyment of the moment itself as well as in the name of helping me grow up as well and productively as possible.

I remember one Chanukah in Boston—I believe it

was a Saturday night, so I was allowed to stay up until ten, a special treat—my present was a miniature hockey game. You moved your players back and forth with a stick in your hand, turned all of them around with that same handle, like in foosball, and tried to score on your opponent. An exciting gift, although there were almost definitely better and more expensive iterations of the game already available.

After the gift-giving, the family had gone to watch some TV show that was not holding my interest. I sat there, eyes drooping, unwilling to go to sleep before the ten o'clock I was promised (what boy goes to sleep *before* he's forced to? Actually, me, as my mother told me many times over the years, but this one night I was resisting).

My father offered a face-saving way out. He would play me one game of hockey, after which I'd go to bed, or I could watch the boring TV show until ten. Of course I chose the game, because with all the discipline, with all the effort to ensure his children would turn out wise and not wicked, I wanted to hang out with my Dad, as we all did.

The Haggadah addresses four of the many kinds of children. In my father's Seder, each kind was to be taken for whom he or she was, and helped to move from *is* to *as good as could be*, with all the considerable skill, energy, and love he could muster.

9:30: *Yachol*, Because I Said So

"Because I said so" were words I hated as a child, but have come to feel more fondness for as a parent. My parents were usually reasonable, patient enough to allow extensive time for discussing or arguing about suggestions or orders. I had to clean up one toy before taking out another so the mess wouldn't pile up, eat my nutritious food first so as to not ruin my appetite with dessert, and all the other rules whose reasons parents explain, to help their children understand the benevolence of the dictatorship in which they live.

Other times, they'd decide my questions were delay tactics, the issue was too simple to be explained again, or they were too rushed to deal with it. Then I'd get the implacable, "Because I said so." To which the only acceptable response was obedience.

When my first child was born, I determined to never say those words; my mother, God bless her, has been granted the revenge of seeing me fail to come close to that goal.

It took me too long to realize that my father's Seder included an example of the balance they struck between patient explanation and "because I said so," an example I had known since my littlest youth, which never sparked the resistance I gave to bedtime or other parental dicta.

This next paragraph of the Haggadah, in fact, is one big "Because I said so."

Our friend the author of the Haggadah wonders whether we might be able to fulfill the *mitzvah* of telling the Exodus story from the beginning of the month. After all, the Jews' first national commandment was to make Nisan the first month, treating the whole month as part of the redemption. If so, perhaps telling the story any time in that month might qualify.

Answers the *Baal Haggadah*, no, the verse that articulates the command to tell the story—the verse we slammed down the throat of the wicked child and used on the one who did not know how to ask—refers to telling the story ביום ההוא, "on that day," the day of our memorial observances of the events.

Perhaps during the day? No, because the verse tells us to tell our children בעבור זה, because of *this*, meaning we should have the appurtenances of the story—the Paschal sacrifice when the Temple stood, and nowadays, the *matzah* and *maror*—physically present while we tell the story. At the Seder, in other words.

It is a perfect example of גזרת הכתוב, Scriptural fiat, Hashem saying "because I said so." Our conclusion isn't that the story only makes sense that night; in fact, we've already seen that it's relevant to mention the Exodus every day of our lives, twice a day. We also never refuted the logic behind telling it from the start of the month or during the day.

Instead, we found a Scriptural ruling that the telling of the story must happen in the presence of *matzah* and *maror*. Because God said so.

Absorbing the rule that I had to listen and obey when God and parents sometimes just said so also prepared me for one of the religious challenges many people do not face until college. After high school, I spent a year at Yeshivat Har Etzion, known as Gush because it is located in the Etzion bloc (Gush in Hebrew) of towns and *kibbutzim*.

My first year back, friends and acquaintances began to struggle with matters of faith. One area of concern was the logic of the commandments which some of these friends, with their full year or two of serious Torah study under their belts, could not find. Why keep commandments that didn't make sense to them?

In my memory—I could be conflating—it was in that environment that R. Aharon Lichtenstein, *zt"l*, one of the two *Roshei Yeshiva* of Yeshivat Har Etzion, visited the US to interview new students and spend Shabbat at Yeshiva University with alumni. As was his practice in *yeshiva* in Israel, he spoke Friday night between *Kabbalat Shabbat*, the service welcoming the Sabbath, and the evening prayers.

The week was *Parashat Parah*, when Jewish communities add a Torah reading about the preparation of a red cow's ashes when the Temple still stood, when rituals of purity and impurity were still daily realities. Those ashes dispel the ritual impurity of contact with a corpse, but render impure the priests who prepare or sprinkle them.

R. Lichtenstein noted a Midrash in which a non-Jew questions R. Yohanan b. Zakkai about this—in some versions, the non-Jew focuses on how ashes can remove impurity at all, in others, he wonders how the same material can create impurity in some and purity in others.

Whatever the prompt, R. Yohanan b. Zakkai quotes Hashem as saying, חוקה חקקתי, גזרה גזרתי אין לכם להרהר אחר גזרותי, "I have legislated a law, decreed a decree, it is not for you to wonder at or question my decrees." Because I said so, from the Master of the Universe.

Perhaps my upbringing prepared me. Perhaps, as with some of my friends, respect for R. Lichtenstein gave his words added authority. Others did not have that reaction. One friend, in fact, ended up abandoning observance. Aside from finding *mitzvot* that did not make sense, Biblical Criticism seemed so logical to him that he became certain the Torah could not have been given at Sinai. Once the foundation crumbled, the rest fell quickly. (Others agree with him intellectually, yet cling to observance for social or cultural reasons. Another story.)

It was one of my first encounters with heresy; I was used to people losing their religion because it was easier to sleep than rise for prayers, to eat anywhere and anything rather than find only kosher places, to join various campus activities on Shabbat rather than restrict themselves to shul and Jewish life, but here was someone leveling logical claims against faith and observance.

Never one to shy away from an intellectual challenge, I began to read the academic literature on his side. There was, also, voluminous literature defending the traditional belief in a Torah completed (at latest) before the passing of Moshe Rabbenu, on the banks of the Jordan. I had no clue as to how to weigh the two. As I had done on other occasions, I went to one of my teachers, and asked him how he dealt with these kinds of concerns.

His answer has been a consistent and important part of my approach to religious texts since, one of the many teachings of his that have shaped my life. I only omit his name because I received the answer in a private conversation and do not know if he would wish to be quoted. He noted that for every text, including but not limited to Torah, meaning comes only in a context; change the context, the meaning changes.

Biblical critics treated Torah like a product of human effort, expecting it to function within the realities of its time, and say only that which a person of that time could have known. By those standards, it could not all have been produced by one author in one period. Traditional scholars read it as a text dictated by God and therefore not subject to the same rules. (Years later, I learned that R. Amital, *zt"l*, the other founding Rosh Yeshiva of Yeshivat Har Etzion, had given a similar answer to R. Mordechai Breuer, *zt"l*, sparking the latter's considerations of Scripture, eventually leading to his famed and original approach to study of those texts.)

The issues raised by Biblical critics were interesting and important, and Gush was one of the places where traditionally-minded Torah scholars were grappling with many of those questions, but their answer started with the divinity of the text.

Choice of contexts, my teacher was pointing out, was the first step. Everything proceeded logically enough from there, on either side.

It was not an answer that satisfied my friend. To me, it had the feeling of home, the warmth of my father's Seder; we believed in the Torah, why? Because Hashem said so.

The Talmud (*Avodah Zarah* 5b) tells us that we don't fully understand our *rebbeim*, our teachers, until after forty years—which, in context, probably means forty years after each lesson. My father's been gone over twenty-five years, but his earliest lessons are now forty years old, and I understand them better day by day, even as I still adhere to some of them (and many of God's) because he or He said so.

9:45: *Mitechillah*, The Greater Freedom of Faith

By this time, the push to move faster had begun in earnest. Because of how my parents spaced their children, there was always a small child whose interest was waning, who needed a rousing rendition of *Dayyenu* and some *matzah* to keep him or her going. We had to book, as we used to say, to keep younger heads in the game.

My father tried to proactively alleviate the problem by dedicating the first night to the first half of the Haggadah, the second night to the second half. It was such a mantra of Pesach in my father's home that I remember the first time we were in Israel for the holiday. Unburdened by exile, we were having only one real Seder (how Americans visiting Israel for a holiday should conduct themselves is an *halachic* discussion of its own, for another time; suffice it to say that that year, my family was going to have a real first Seder and a second one *pro forma*).

My first reaction was that there was no way one could say all we needed to in just one night. I had to consciously remind myself that God only asked for one Seder, so apparently the commandment could be fulfilled in that time frame.

At my father's Seder, it was no solution for another reason. Time after time, we found so many irresistible comments on the first half that, even on the night dedicated to the second half, we still reached this paragraph, the halfway point, way behind. Every Seder *had* to have a retelling of how the rabbis in Benei Berak were considering a rebellion, of how R. Elazar b. Azaryah's beard went gray. It couldn't be otherwise.

Pressed for time as we were starting to feel, we also were about to hit one of the best parts of my father's Seder. This next piece of the Haggadah, which recalls that our forefathers were idol-worshippers, is included because of a Talmudic debate about the focus of the recounting of the Exodus. The more intuitive opinion held that the story should consist of עבדים היינו, "we were slaves to Pharaoh," the paragraph we said right after the Four Questions. The Exodus is when we left Egypt, so we recall the slavery in Egypt.

The other opinion sends us back to Abraham, who built a nation on the foundation of rejection of worship of any being other than Hashem. The physical act of leaving Egypt was also the moment when God brought us close, as a nation, to His service, and that was the real Exodus.

I was a young teen when I came across the ArtScroll Haggadah, which packaged a wealth of traditional sources in an English format I could glide through easily. Their commentary first made explicit that the two views differed on whether the Pesach Seder primarily celebrated the physical or spiritual freedom. What the ArtScroll didn't point out, but my father lived out at his Seder, was that the *Baal Haggadah* puts most of the story after we get to this paragraph.

Other than the bare-bones statement that we were slaves and saved, the Haggadah so far has discussed why we're telling the story, how much to tell, how to tailor it to our listeners, when to tell it. It's only now, after mentioning the spiritual side, the Exodus bringing us to Hashem's worship, that we expound and expand upon verses that tell the story, however briefly.

That subtle emphasis on the religious side of the Exodus became not so subtle in my relationship with my father a few years later, when we had a conversation whose significance he may not have realized, but became a cornerstone of my personal development. We were sitting in the kitchen in the Brooklyn house, the one I think of as my parents' house, where they lived for twelve years before my father passed away and where my mother stayed for around another twelve before selling it.

It may have been a Friday night after everyone else went to sleep, but it may equally have been some other time when we happened to be alone together in the kitchen. I was sitting on one of the cane chairs at the table in the breakfast area, he was over past the refrigerator, making himself coffee out of the hot water urn or browsing the snack closet above that. I was in my late teens, I think, not rebellious, just wondering about the certainty of faith he exuded.

There we were, I figured I'd ask. "What makes you believe in God?"

He looked over and gave me an answer I later found out had been given many times before, most famously in the *Kuzari*, R. Judah ha-Levi's eleventh-century work of Jewish thought. It was new to me, and in that moment my father turned it into an heirloom.

213

"Because my father told me that his father told him, and his father told him, and so on, that one of our direct ancestors stood at Sinai and heard God give the Torah."

Simple as he made it sound, it is anything but. There is significant debate, in traditional Jewish circles, as to what exactly the people heard at Sinai; others deny the persuasive value in a claim to have witnessed and experienced prophecy (although it is an almost-unique claim in human history, and certainly unique among any of the major religions, that the entirety of a people witnessed revelation).

For me, that night and since, none of that mattered. My father was telling me that in our family, we know God exists—the God of Creation, of the Exodus, of the Giving of the Law and the Revelation at Sinai, of *halachah*, Jewish law—because we met Him.

Years later, I read an article in which R. Joseph B. Soloveitchik, *zt"l*, tells the story of his first meeting with Maimonides, the Rambam. As he put it, "How did I come to know the Rambam? We met." In his boyhood home, he went on to relate, his father taught a late evening class once a week, aiming at uncovering the logic and reason in various of Rambam's claims, some abstruse. The child Rav—genius though he was—could not follow the discussion, other than to see if his father had saved the Rambam from those who questioned or attacked his positions.

When he did, the boy would run to his mother excitedly, to tell her that his father had saved the Rambam. When the father failed, the son would sadly report that to his mother as well. She would comfort him by suggesting that maybe one day he himself would save the Rambam.

The story's charms are many and obvious; for me, there was a whiff of familiarity as well. In that very learned family, they met the Rambam at a young age. In my family, we remembered that we had met Hashem, long ago, and we would stick with that.

The conversation came back to me when I found myself eulogizing my father outside a dark cemetery in Beit Shemesh on the fifth night of Chanukah. My words at his funeral in Brooklyn took a whole night of tears to prepare. I had not thought I'd speak again. The cemetery is located near enough to follow the custom of Jerusalem and bury even at night. When we arrived, there were many more people than I expected, gathered to perform this final kindness for my father—in the middle of Chanukah, a time of festivity and rejoicing.

One of my *rebbeim*, my teachers from *yeshiva*, suggested I say something, to give the people, some of whom did not know my father, who had come because they knew me or one of my siblings, some sense of whom we had lost. What I had said in Brooklyn did not fit, and I had moments to prepare, not the whole night I had had to shape my first attempt to bid him a proper farewell.

The conversation in the kitchen, that's what came to me. When I had to pick out one gift he had given me, among the many, when I had to thank him one last time for all he had done, it was the gift of faith, the bedrock knowledge that, however it works, whatever philosophical problems challenge us, my family (like all Jews, but he was the one who passed this to me) knew God, because it's a staple of our family inheritance.

Because מתחילה עובדי עבודה זרה היו אבותינו, "at first our forefathers were idol-worshippers," but now the Lord has brought us close to His service. As my father did for me, at that Seder and throughout his life.

Pushing 10:00: *Arami Oved Avi*, The Room My Father Left for Me to Succeed

It was late, there was a ways to go, and this next section of the Haggadah was even more textually focused than the others, far beyond the capabilities of the younger set. Yet it is also one of the oldest sections, mentioned in Mishnah *Pesachim* 10:4.

The Mishnah says to be דורש this section, "to analyze it intensively," yet reading just the verses and added points in the Haggadah takes time, let alone trying to understand the workings of those derivations and the points being made.

I would be hungry, already flipping forward to check what was left. We had four verses to expound, the Plagues to review, a series of claims about how many plagues there were, in Egypt and at the Sea, *Dayyenu* to sing (we *had* to sing *Dayyenu*, even on the nights of first-half focus, even if we were terribly late), the three observances of the Seder to note, and then we'd be at the second cup, *matzah, maror,* and the meal. A lot.

So we were seriously behind the eight-ball, and the *kneidel*, the matzoh balls, were waiting to be put into the soup. First, that meant my father, prodded by my mother and the youngest at the table, would urge us to move faster, to bring up only those ideas or questions that were absolutely necessary, and, worst of all, to refrain from jokes.

That time pressure made *Arami Oved Avi* undeniably the section given shortest shrift at my father's Seder. It is, for one thing, more technical. The verses the Talmud says to analyze are from Deut. 26:5-8, part of the ceremony for bringing first fruits, בכורים, to Jerusalem. To celebrate the harvest, the Torah told Jews to bring the first fruits from the seven species for which the Land of Israel was praised to the Temple. Before handing them over to a priest, the Jew would recite these verses, which summarize the Exodus, as a lead-in to thanking God for the bounty of the Land given to the Jewish people.

The *Baal Haggadah* offers expositions of each of the phrases. For some, he cites the verse in Exodus that shows that events occurred as we say them in Deuteronomy. For example, when we say ויענונו, "they made us suffer," the Haggadah refers us to Exod. 1:11, that the Egyptians assigned taskmasters to oppress us in our labors.

Other times, the Haggadah gives added insight into the original text. When Deut. 26:8 speaks of Hashem taking us out of Egypt ביד חזקה, "with a strong hand," the Haggadah points us to Exod. 9:3, where the plague of pestilence is referred to as the Hand of Hashem. That's not to prove there *was* a strong hand; it's a claim about what aspect of the Exodus *constituted* that hand (so, too, when the Haggadah understands עמלנו, "our sufferings," to refer to the sons the Egyptians threw in the river).

It was too late for any length on any of this, but my father always clarified the basic meaning, making sure we knew whether the supporting verse proved what had happened or expanded upon it, and how the prooftext did or did not clarify the verse. Reading and understanding, at a basic level, was the bare minimum for the Seder.

That was a truth taken so for granted that years later it was a shock to realize some people don't bother reading the entire Haggadah. I once served as a rabbi at a hotel for Passover, where I had to run a central Seder. I was told, sternly, that the attendees did not want a long Seder, they wanted to get to the meal. The first night, I did my best but took too long.

The second night, I read the words as quickly as I could with barely a brief English summary. I went so fast, family members warned me I would annoy people. They were wrong; everyone loved it.

That wasn't the surprise. The surprise was when I went into the main dining room while the waiters set up the meal. Everyone there ran their own Seder, and I found that many of them were also already at or beyond the meal. Meaning they gone faster than me, even though I was barely reading and translating!

The *Arami Oved Avi* section became for me, in later years, a gap in my father's legacy, the great white he never bagged, the one he left me to reel in. He always expected and hoped I would go him one better (as I do with my children). I learned that from him implicitly, then learned it from *Chullin* 6b in my first year away from home. R. Yehudah ha-Nasi, the editor of the Mishnah, decides that Beit Shean was outside of Israel, with several *halachic* ramifications.

When his father's family objected that he was deviating from their longstanding custom, he adduced Scriptural proofs to show that our forefathers leave us room to grow, excel, and even supersede them in some ways.

Arami Oved Avi is one of the places he left me to work on. I can't say I've succeeded, but each year I pay particular attention to this section, hoping to find a way to make its messages clear and interesting enough to all those at my Seder.

Here, as I try to recapture his Seder, I will leave *Arami Oved Avi* as he did, rushed through without any particular exposition. Except for the one joke we always told. It was from my father's Uncle Ignatz, and took me years to remember. Once I had gotten it down, I didn't want to lose it.

To understand, you have to know about Uncle Ignatz, one of my grandmother's two never-married brothers, who lived near her in Washington. He had apparently been a brilliant scientist—his sisters often spoke of how Einstein had read his dissertation and sent a laudatory letter—but by the time I knew him, he was more than a little eccentric. Pleasant enough company, always eager for good conversation and humor, but not quite up to the challenges of daily life.

This section of the Haggadah refers to Hashem seeing our various afflictions in Egypt, including את עמלנו, "our (futile) toils." While the simplest meaning might have been the work they imposed upon us, the *Baal Haggadah* comments אלו הבנים, "these are the sons," the male babies the Egyptians threw in the river. Futile toil, indeed, to become pregnant, carry a child for nine months, go through labor and childbirth, and then have the newborn taken away and drowned!

The year I recall having Seder with Uncle Ignatz—the same year my other relative replaced the *afikoman* I had stolen, a banner Seder all around—he lapsed into German, so I missed the joke completely. All the adults laughed, though, so I asked what he had said. My father explained that he had said אלו הבנים, "these are the sons," and then named several early leaders of the Reform movement in Germany whose names ended with *sohn*, German for "son."

It was a joke that recurred at our Seder precisely because I did not understand it until long after. For all the intervening years, I'd stop my father at that point, and say, "What was that joke Uncle Ignatz told?" needing to have it explained to me all over again.

Not a great joke, but that was as far as we got with *Arami Oved Avi*, at least at my father's Seder. Leaving room for me and the rest of his descendants to add our pieces to the family legacy.

10:15: Plagues and Watching the Downfall of Evil

From my younger years, a moment of respite. This Seder was tiring. Bedtime was serious business for my parents—it was 7:30 until fifth grade, when they conceded that a new city, with a new school and more homework, meant I'd have to be allowed to stay up until eight. Whatever the bedtime (until late in high school, when it fell apart, me too old and they too busy to police it), this night was *much* later than I was used to (even with the mandatory pre-Seder nap), and I was expected to be keeping up with all this reading and understanding as well!

Worse, from the first cup—other than the barely-stomached radishes—it had been reading and talking, with only a smattering of singing back at *Mah Nishtanah* and *Avadim Hayinu*. Enjoyable, but by this point, especially after the rush of derivations of *Arami Oved Avi*, I was ready for a change of pace.

The Plagues gave us a ritual, an *action*. Like in homes all over the world, we hovered our pinkies over our cups and, as we formally intoned each Plague, knocked a bit of grape juice out of the cup onto the small plate underneath. Then we sucked whatever liquid was left, a small but welcome infusion of sugar.

The price was explaining each plague, a bit of a challenge since I always mixed up wild animals with locusts (ערוב and ארבה, pronounced *arov* and *arbeh*, fairly close to each other) and lice and locusts, two 'l' words that described insects with which I had no personal experience.

That hurdle leaped, we moved on to R. Yehudah, a rabbi from the time of the Mishnah (second century CE), who gave an acronym for the ten, taking the first letters of each plague and turning it into three words (דצ״ך עד״ש באח״ב). For each word of the acronym, we knocked a bit more grape juice out of the cup.

In some homes, the Plagues were a highlight, an opportunity to involve the littlest children by pulling out toys, playacting, in general giving the table a chance to move around, shake off a bit of the intensity of analysis until that point.

We had some of that—the youngest were always anxious to show that they knew the translation of each plague, and their excitement over finding a way back into the center of the action was infectious. Still, the Plagues never took deep root in my father's Seder. We never skipped them, and I enjoyed the grape juice I got to lick off my finger, meager as it was, but we never got much thrill out of them, either.

I think the explanation we give for spilling some grape juice also shows why the Plagues just couldn't do it for us at my father's Seder. It's well known that we reduce the drink in our cups out of sorrow that the Egyptians had to suffer. Our cups, literal and metaphorical, cannot be completely full when our good fortune is built off Egyptian misfortune, however deserved.

Many see that as the explanation for not reciting all of *Hallel* after the first day of Pesach (or two, outside of Israel) of Pesach, as opposed to Sukkot, when we say Psalms 113-118 straight through for all the days of the holiday.

The Talmud offers a technical reason based on the additional sacrifices brought in the Temple on each of those days, but the Midrash has it that when the angels attempted to sing praises after the Splitting of the Sea, Hashem stopped them, saying, מעשי ידי טובעים בים ואתם אומרים שירה, "the work of My hands are drowning in the Sea, and you recite songs of praise?"

The Jews were allowed to sing because they were celebrating salvation, not expressing joy at the suffering of others. We, too, limit our praises to the first day, to empathize with the sorrows the Egyptians brought upon themselves. Once you know that, there seemed little reason to dwell upon these Plagues; they were worth knowing, part of the Pesach story, but certainly no focus of the night.

I might have thought this sadness at others' troubles, however deserved, would have been a harder message to convey in a home touched by World War II. My father was born in 1938 in Yugoslavia, fled to Italy when he was three, where the family spent three years moving around to avoid detection and deportation.

I had heard about those years growing up, but it became more real after he passed away, when I went through his papers in search of his will. I came across a form he had filled out for a job in the early 1960's which involved some government work (to my lasting chagrin, I neglected to keep the form, and it is now lost forever). It was the first time I had seen an official document bearing a version of the theretofore mythical question, "Are you now or have you ever been a member of the Communist Party?"

It was less romantic on the piece of paper my father had kept, since it asked, "Are you now or have you ever been a member of any of the groups listed in Section A or B below," and then listed some 15-20 versions of the Communist and other undesirable Parties of the time.

He was also asked to list all the places he had lived, and there were almost ten for the three years he'd been in Italy. I had known those years were hard, had heard the stories of my father and aunt sharing an egg as his birthday present one year. There was never any suggestion they had gone through anything similar to what "real" Holocaust survivors had endured, but it wasn't as if they had escaped unscathed.

They lost all their money, which cannot compare to their lives, but does matter. My grandfather had been one of the pillars of the Jewish community of Zagreb, financially as well as by serving as president. I recall the family receiving a reparations check in the mid-1980's for the furnishings in their apartment, of about $6000. It didn't impress me until my father noted, with more irony than bitterness (we were comfortable by then), that the Yugoslavian government had cut a check for the 1930's valuation of the items, without adjusting for inflation or the fifty years the family had had to go without.

Losing your social and financial status, never to get it back, wears on you, even if others had it immeasurably worse. My grandfather passed away, after four heart attacks, when I was too young to remember him. Near as I can tell, he never found himself in the United States, scraping along—with significant help from my grandmother, a certified dentist in Europe who worked the rest of her life as a hygienist because she did not have time, with children to support, to spend two years retraining to US standards to re-enter the profession she had previously plied.

But they survived, had a third child, and all three grew up safe and healthy, went to college, started professions, and had families of their own. Still, had they been bitter towards Germans, Croats, or even non-Jews in general, many of whom were complicit with the Nazis in ways large and small, I would have understood. That your suffering is minor in comparison to others doesn't make it insignificant.

The Plagues, at the Seder, would have been the perfect time to vent a little. Some *schadenfreude*, a bit of glee at watching those who injured us get what they had coming, wouldn't have been out of place.

That was not my father's way. If I have to reconstruct his perspectives of non-Jews, I cannot, because there was no such monolith in our family. My father was, in this, the embodiment of the mathematician in the story he enjoyed telling, of an engineer, a physicist, and a mathematician traveling on a train through Scotland, and seeing some black sheep.

The engineer says, "Oh, sheep in Scotland are black." The physicist corrects him, that all they know is that there are *some* black sheep in Scotland. The mathematician trumps his rigor, pointing out that they only know that Scotland has some sheep that are black *on one side.*

My father never gave a free pass to evil, Jewish or not, but equally refused to paint with too broad a brush. Other than the Germans alive and active during WWII—whose penitence never convinced him—he did not speak of non-Jews as a unit. There were good and heroic non-Jews, in Europe during the war and in the United States, a country whose welcome to Jews he never underestimated.

At the same time there were, sadly, non-Jews who acted in an evil way. There was no point whitewashing their deeds, and they were to be resisted, fought against ferociously, but only as long as they insisted on that course of action.

Plagues were plagues, sometimes necessary but never the best way for the world to work. True in real life, it was true in our Seder as well.

10:25: Counting Plagues in Egypt and at the Sea

We were in the homestretch. I had grape juice on my tongue, could feel *matzah* waiting to be eaten. Yet the *Baal Haggadah* managed to pack in three last bits of enduring impact. First, there was the Mishnaic discussion, debate, or competition over which rabbi could find more plagues that befell the Egyptians.

It started with R. Yosi ha-Gelili (of Galilee), who noted that while there were ten in Egypt, there were fifty at the Splitting of the Sea, a number he derived from Scripture's noting that the Jews saw God's great Hand against the Egyptians. In Egypt, Pharaoh's sorcerers had conceded that the Plagues were the finger of God, and that was ten, so that the Hand of God should signal fifty plagues.

My father would note that R. Yosi ha-Gelili assumed that when the sorcerers reacted to the third plague, lice, by saying it was the finger of God, they meant the plagues as a phenomenon, not lice in particular. Otherwise the math didn't work.

There were, of course, holes in this logic that we discussed from time to time, such as how R. Yosi knew the sorcerers were right to characterize the plagues as a finger, and his certainty that the Biblical metaphors of finger and hand indicated a mathematical translation into numbers of plagues.

But we never got too critical about R. Yosi, since the other two rabbis the Haggadah cites, R. Eliezer and R. Akiva, accepted his assumptions, that whatever happened at the Sea was five times as bad as what had happened in Egypt.

Where they argued was how bad it was in Egypt. Granted that the book of Exodus speaks of ten Plagues, R. Eliezer notes that Psalm 78:49 describes Hashem's sending those plagues with the words ישלח בם חרון אפו, "He inflicted His burning anger upon them," elaborating on that with the words עברה וזעם צרה משלחת מלאכים רעים, "wrath, indignation, trouble, band of deadly messengers."

For R. Eliezer, those four further terms meant that each plague was four plagues, making a total of forty plagues in Egypt and two hundred at the Sea. R. Akiva cited the same verse but argued that each plague was five, giving us fifty and two hundred fifty.

Among the questions raised by the passage, my father's Seder focused on two: first, what interested him most, how did they read the same verse to such different ends? Second, what does it mean that each plague "was" four or five plagues?

He would make sure we understood that R. Eliezer and R. Akiva were, at bedrock, arguing about how to read the verse. R. Eliezer assumed that Hashem inflicted "burning anger" upon the Egyptians, which is then characterized by the adjectives to come. Wrath, indignation, and so on were expressions of the burning anger.

R. Akiva instead read burning anger as the first in the list of that which Hashem inflicted upon them. While many today would assume they were predisposed to find four or five elements of each plague, that their inclinations shaped their reading, my father always gave the impression that the first step, for us and for them, was textual analysis. Only after we understand the text on its own terms can we come to further conclusions.

The ramifications for this instance became clearer with his noting that these two rabbis were telling us that the verse meant that each plague had multiple aspects. They weren't just blood, or frogs, or lice, they were blood, frogs, or lice administered with wrath and indignation. For R. Eliezer, each plague had four terrible and terrifying aspects; for R. Akiva, five.

My father was oddly uninterested in my main concern: why were they doing this? Even if the verse implied all this, what was the point or value in squabbling over exactly how many plagues, or aspects of plagues, the Egyptians suffered? Why did our vaunted *Baal Haggadah* include this in our busy night?

I think my father's answer was that it makes the miracle greater, that by this point in the Haggadah, closing in on the brief songs of praise before the meal, we cite rabbinic sources that magnified the wonders God had wrought. Having spoken of enslavement and its burdens, plagues and the redemption, we indulge in a little hyperbole.

This was not the kind of answer that would usually satisfy him. Perhaps textual concerns distracted him, the insight that חרון אפו has an ambiguous place in that verse. Or perhaps the math sidetracked him. By the time I was born, my father had been working in computers for several years. That was in the early 1960's, when computer technology was a really young field; in classic Rothstein fashion, instead of sticking with it and its frustrations, where he might have risen to both prominence and wealth as the field grew, he left in 1971 to start all over in law.

But, growing up, I don't remember being told that he worked in computers, that he was a systems analyst; I remember being told he was a mathematician. He had started out at Brooklyn College at night—while in Chaim Berlin, a *yeshiva*, during the day, part of the reason my decision to attend Yeshiva University went over better with him than it might have—and spent a year at the Courant Institute, getting a Master's.

Then, in my mother's telling, he realized or decided he would never make a mark in math, and moved on to computers. He may have switched professionally, from math to computers to corporate law, to real estate, to tax, but he never lost his love of math.

Early in my struggles with calculus, he came upon me one time—head in my hands, trying to figure out the impenetrable textbook. I looked up, hair mussed from my hand tearing at it (ahh, the days of hair!). He asked what I was doing and, when I told him, said, "Oh, yes, that's the calculus pose."

He had a wistful fondness for those halcyon days. Then he spent that year freaking me out, re-deriving the calculus at our Shabbat meals. He'd ask me what I was working on; by this point, I was old enough to remember something. I'd mention an idea that had struck me as interesting, and he wouldn't let me finish. Instead, he'd take the kernel I mentioned and find his way to the answer—always taking a route other than I had been taught, making me sure he'd gone wrong, only to have him end up at the right place, pleased with himself, but more, pleased with the math.

I don't know if he ever realized the extent of his joy and enjoyment. He once told me he hadn't understood what a derivative was until his second year of calculus, when he walked into class one day and the professor had posted a definition that made it all clear. Not loving calculus nearly as much as he did (I never took a math course beyond the calculus my high school offered), I asked him the obvious: if you didn't understand a derivative, what would make you take a *second* year?

He had no convincing answer, leaving me to put two and two together: he loved math, and this was the next step. He never could explain what he liked so much about it, since he was a man who lived true love, not described it.

This left me the only one of us troubled by these rabbis' apparently meaningless mental gymnastics. Which might be why I was the one who found the answer that joined our Seder forever after. I learned it in elementary school, ascribed to the Vilna Gaon, R. Elijah Kramer of Vilna, a legendary eighteenth-century figure, stories about whom have filled enough other volumes that I can leave it at that.

The Gaon ("genius," in Hebrew) linked this discussion to the promise in Exod. 15:26, that if we listen to God and do that which is right in His eyes, all the מחלה, all the illness or troubles that Hashem had placed upon the Egyptians, He would not place upon us. Commentators have expatiated on that at length; the Gaon teased out only the implication that the more plagues, illnesses, and troubles that had hit the Egyptians, the broader our immunity, should we listen to Hashem and do that which he wanted.

This gave a positive effect to the textual reading and mathematical contortions, which appealed to both of us, and became one more place my father allowed my contributions to change his Seder.

10:30: *Dayenu*

Of course we sang *Dayenu* at my father's Seder. What self-respecting home *doesn't* sing *Dayenu*? With more gusto than melody. As we sang it, the tune didn't fit the words, not beyond the first line. So we'd start off strong, אלו הוציא הוציאנו, הוציאנו ממצרים, *ilu hotsi, hotsianu, hotsianu mi-Mitsrayim*, but soon after it would become a Procrustean exercise, stuffing more words into a line than could fit, or stretching out the few available ones to last the needed notes.

The chorus, repeating the word *Dayenu* over and over, was spirit-renewing, and my father played it up for the youngest among us, who had had to tolerate over an hour of conversation that was beyond them.

The word appears at the end of each line, but there was no way we could sing a full chorus that many times. Checking his watch and his patience, my father would, after the end of the first chorus, say, "Every fourth," or, if we had extra time that year, "every third." The last line always had room for a "one more time," or, on the second night, for another time, "last time for this year."

We enjoyed it, but the next piece of the Haggadah explained to me part of why music on its own never did it for my father. The song says that had Hashem only done *x*,

Dayenu, literally, "it would have been enough for us." My father's Seder favored the explanations of "enough" that either that would already have been all we merited or that that alone would have been an experience worth having. Then we move on to another wonder that also would have been *Dayenu*, enough.

Right after the song, we say על אחת כמה וכמה, "how much more so," that Hashem has done all these wonders for us, and list them again, emphasizing the gratitude we owe for His having done all that—taking us out of Egypt, destroying their gods, killing their first-born, on to the end of the list, through giving Shabbat, bringing us to Sinai, giving the Torah, Israel, and building the Temple in Jerusalem.

Song or no song, at my father's Seder, we went through the list carefully, analyzing and explaining the importance of each of the items. Even later that night, my father sometimes dozing through the post-Seder songs, he would rouse himself enough to check that we knew what we were singing, what we were saying. A spoonful of music helped the message go down, he might have said, but it was the words that counted.

True at the Seder, I remember first noticing words of a song on a Friday night sometime in elementary school. That week, my class had learned the story of Yosef מוקיר שבת, Yosef who loved the Sabbath. In the Talmudic tale, the poor Yosef stretched himself week after week, despite his poverty, to find something special for Shabbat.

His rich, evil neighbor mocked him for his efforts. Then a soothsayer predicted that the neighbor's wealth would all go to Yosef one day. Determined to foil the prediction, the wealthy man converted all his assets into jewels, sewed them into the lining of a hat (to keep with him at all times), and sailed for a distant land. As he was congratulating himself for outwitting his fate, a strong wind blew the hat off his head, into the sea, where it was swallowed by a large fish.

Meanwhile, Yosef had been having an unusually hard week, barely scraping by. Late in the day on Friday, he finally found the money to buy fish for Shabbat. Rushing to the market, he found a huge one, freshly caught, that the press of time (before refrigeration, everything had to be sold or it would go bad; as Shabbat approached, prices dropped) had put in his price range.

Hurrying home, he gave the fish to his wife to clean and cook. She sliced it open only to gasp at the hat inside, loaded with enough jewels to make them wealthy for the rest of their lives!

It's a classic mold: a saintly hero suffering privations until he comes to his deserved rewards of wealth and comfort, a cartoonish villain receiving his comeuppance. But I was a kid, and didn't know that yet. More, that Friday night, I suddenly recognized some of the words in my father's favorite *zemer*, Friday night song, the one he always sang while the soup was being served—יוסף חצה דג ומצא מרגליות בבשרו, "Yosef split a fish and found precious stones in its flesh."

Wait a minute, I remember thinking, I *know* that story. And once I was looking, I knew another story in the song, the one about two angels following Jews home from synagogue Friday night, checking whether the house was well-prepared. If it was, the good angel would bless them that the next week should look the same; if not, the bad angel would curse them that the next week should look the same (karma's a beast, or something like that). The other angel would have to answer amen.

There it was in my father's song: ואם שלחן כדת ערוך ומלאך א-ל יענה ברוך...ומלאך רע יענה אמן, בעל כרחו יספר שבחו, "if the table is set properly, the angel of good will pronounce a blessing... and the evil angel will answer amen, against his (the angel's) will, he will tell his praises!"

The song was replete with references to Talmudic ideas about Shabbat and its wonders. For my father and me, it had the perfect ratio of tune (if we can call it that) to content. Occasionally, at others' homes, when I was asked if I knew a *zemer* I wished to share, I would go with that one, leaving my hosts unsure as to whether it *had* a tune.

The song gave new insight even after my father's passing. While studying for my graduate school exams, in a book on the Jewish view of copyright by Nahum Rackover, I found the story of the author of this song, R. Yehonatan of Lunel (1100's in Provence), arriving at a town, only to find that the local cantor was passing it off as his own creation.

In those days, proving ownership of intellectual property might have been impossible, except that this man had stolen the song a bit early. R. Yehonatan challenged the impostor to demonstrate how they could tell that the song was unfinished, and then finish it. When he couldn't, R. Yehonatan showed the townspeople it was an acrostic, spelling out Yehonatan (his name) and the first two letters of the word חזק, strong, a common way of closing an acrostic. He then composed the last stanza, completing the acrostic, and focused it on a call for others to stay away from his property. A fun story to distract from a tough year, and my father's song offered it.

When I married, I had wanted the *benchers*—booklets placed on the tables, so that guests can recite the Grace After Meals; many have Shabbat songs as well—to include the song. We couldn't find any that were in the right range of price and beauty, so I relented, made do without.

Almost two decades later, preparing for the Bar Mitzvah of our first son, the one named after my father, my wife found and bought *benchers* based on their cover, but the song was also inside. Once my father's namesake reached adulthood, the song returned to our house.

The fatalist in my father would have enjoyed the seeming coincidence—a view of life partially captured in one of his favorite stories, the frontispiece to the novel *Appointment in Samarra*. It seems a certain Arab's favorite servant came home one day, flustered, and asked his master for his fastest camel. The master asked why, and the servant explained that he had just been walking in the market, and seen Death, and Death had looked at him strangely; the servant begged for the camel that he might flee to Samarra, to avoid Death.

The master gave him the camel, and then went to the marketplace himself, where he accosted Death. "What are you doing, scaring my servant like that?"

Death apologized. "I did not mean to; I was just surprised to see him here. You see, I have an appointment with him tomorrow. In Samarra."

Words, like those of *Dayenu*, that were music to my father's ears.

10:45: Rabban Gamliel's Three Statements

After all that back-and-forth, the potpourri and plethora of different types of Torah thoughts and songs, the 10:30 mark frequently already far in the past, Rabban Gamliel comes along to warn us we still might not have achieved the minimum required for the *mitzvah*. Unless we mention the Paschal sacrifice, *matzah*, and *maror*, the three food appurtenances of the Seder, we have not fulfilled our basic obligation.

Even to a young child, that was odd. Here we are, a good hour and a half into doing nothing but thinking and speaking about Hashem's saving us from slavery, and Rabban Gamliel would tell us we hadn't done the job right? We had taken two approaches to the story, remember, spoken of the physical and spiritual redemption, had expounded the Torah's own encapsulation in *Arami Oved Avi*, and Rabban Gamliel was telling us we hadn't fulfilled the basic mitzvah?!

It was an easy way to learn what my father stressed in other places, that sincerity is not enough. Pesach night, you could spend as much or more time than we had, you could throw yourself into speaking of the Exodus, and still miss not just a הידור, a beautifying element of the *mitzvah*, but an essential, indispensable one. Sure, Hashem would see and you'd get credit for sincerity, but that would not be the same as having fulfilled the *mitzvah*.

It was so basic to my upbringing that I am always surprised to meet people who do not see it, who have not been nursed on my father's milk of understanding that what we do is as or more important as how sincerely we wanted to act well. When I did something wrong by accident, and I would protest, "But I didn't mean it!" He would say, "You should mean it, yet?"

The corollary is that legal niceties often matter very much, whether or not we see how they play into the underlying goal. This comes up often today, since some attempts at innovation in Jewish practice pay insufficient attention to those legal niceties. If the outcome appears good, some of us think, there has to be a way to get to it.

One early example, for me, was an op-ed in the *New York Times* by a woman whose half-sister, the product of her mother's second marriage, had moved to Israel and was looking to marry. Unless the first marriage had been dissolved in an *halachically* valid manner, the second marriage—regardless of and despite the parties' intentions—counts as an adulterous affair, and any child is a *mamzer(et)*, forbidden from marrying most Jews.

The problem became more prevalent in the late 20th century, when divorce rates rose, many of those divorces occurring without requisite rabbinic supervision, producing civilly but not *halachically* recognized divorces.

One way to help children of these second marriages avoid the eternal stigma of *mamzerut*, loosely translated as *halachic* illegitimacy, is to invalidate the first marriage, to show that that first wedding had not followed the necessary procedure to produce an *halachic* union. That means that, by Jewish law, the first couple lived together out of wedlock, and their children were born out of wedlock, which—crucially—does not render them illegitimate.

This process clears the children of the second marriage of a debilitating permanent blemish, since their mother had never been married, and was thus not engaged in an adulterous affair (from the perspective of Jewish law) with their father. Sticklers could find some issue with a child born out of wedlock, but Jewish law does not see it as anywhere near as problematic as in popular culture and imagination, so this solution saves the children of the second marriage without—again, by the standards of Jewish law—causing anything approaching that damage to the children of the first marriage.

The woman writing the op-ed could not see the difference. As a product of the first marriage, she wrote plaintively, complaining that when her mother signed the document, it declared that her child born out of wedlock was illegitimate.

But only from an *halachic* perspective, I wanted to yell at the newspaper in my hands. From an American perspective, her parents had been legally married and divorced, so she was not born out of wedlock, and, from an *halachic* perspective, her parents' marital status when she was conceived had little bearing on her personal status.

She needed a good dose of Rabban Gamliel—you can spend a whole night on a story, but you also have to fulfill the legal niceties. Caught up in one worldview, she could not see the legal needs of another.

Or, a Pesach question: two people are at a Seder; one, in a rush, takes some *matzah* and eats it, quickly and unthinkingly, not paying attention to its deeper ramifications as a vehicle of reminding us of the Seder story. (*Matzah* is one of Rabban Gamliel's three items, so his telling of the Seder story would be lacking, but I am speaking about the commandment to eat *matzah*.)

Another person, with all the best intent in the world, lovingly considers the symbolism of *matzah*, the role it played in the Jews' early national experience, and then, with great intent and attention, eats an apple (he or she doesn't like *matzah*). Which of the two has come closer to fulfilling the *mitzvah* to eat *matzah* that night?

Having grown up at my father's Seder, the answer is obvious, but it is not obvious to everyone. Many of us have become so focused on intent, internal experience, and personal growth, that we cannot see the difference between fulfilling a commanded action and doing a different, but similar, one. That was one of the gifts Rabban Gamliel gave me—an awareness, early on, of the existence of minimal standards independent of intent, concern, devotion, enthusiasm, or any other mental state.

His second point was, for me, even more formative, and even more subtly so. Because, at least at my father's Seder, Rabban Gamliel did not only tell us that these three items had to be linked to the Seder story—the Paschal sacrifice, the *matzah*, and the *maror*—he told us that, in some sense, these three items captured the Seder story. What we had been doing until now was all well and good, but these three items focused us on the bare essentials of the story. Whatever deficiencies there had been in our telling until now, we could make them up by pointing at these three items and telling their tale.

The *maror* brought to mind the bitterness of the enslavement, the Paschal sacrifice reminded us of the salvation, and the *matzah*—in Rabban Gamliel's presentation—was a reminder of how quickly we left Egypt. The whole story, in three easy steps.

As I grew to recognize how impossible it would be for me to ever come to know the whole of Torah, or even a significant portion of it, my mind turned to finding the most essential pieces, those texts and ideas that captured what Rabban Gamliel had for the Seder, the bare minimum to have accomplished something meaningful. Whatever time I was putting in, I wanted to know I was working on that which was most necessary.

Similarly, as I grew to recognize that I would never fulfill all the *mitzvot* despite my continuing efforts to improve at doing so, my mind turned to ensuring I paid most attention to the most significant ones. That also translated into an educational question: granted that most students—young and old—will absorb only a small percentage of what rabbis try to convey, which are the most essential?

It all started at my father's Seder, when he passed down Rabban Gamliel's insight, that even with a lot of effort, even with a population clearly interested in doing the most they can, there were legal niceties to be met, which could be best accomplished by offering an essentialist version, to make sure that nothing vital was lost in the rush to do as much as possible.

10:55: Binding the Generations: *Bechol Dor va-Dor*, Second Cup, *Matzah, Maror, Korech*

We're almost there. At my father's Seder, we had arrived at the words that would later start me on a continuing goal, making sure we succeed at fulfilling the Haggadah's requirement (from Mishnah *Pesachim* 10:5), that בכל דור ודור, in every generation a Jew has to see him/herself as if personally leaving Egypt, with those exact feelings. Part of sharing my father's Seder has been in the hope that watching how he guided my siblings and me to that point might be helpful or productive for you.

This point in the Seder was and is the test of our success. When I was younger, all I cared about was how late I could tell my friends we had gone. As I grew to be more aware of the Seder's mandate to live in real time as well as historical time, I grew to see that we need to live life while also, a few times a year, reliving what happened long ago as if it were the present. It is not enough to *believe* in the Exodus, I had heard from forever, we have to *live* it once a year.

R. Soloveitchik once described his *shiurim*, his Talmud classes, with a finely honed sense of the mixing of the two kinds of time. He said:

Whenever I start the *shiur*, the door opens, another old man walks in and sits down... Rav Hayyim Brisker, without whom you cannot learn nowadays. The door opens quietly again and another old man walks in... Shabbesai Cohen, the famous Shakh who must be present when *dinei mamonot* are discussed... More visitors show up ...Rabbi Akiva, Rashi, Rabbenu Tam, the Ra'avad, the Rashba, more and more come in. What do I do? I introduce them to my pupils and the dialogue commences.

The Rambam says something and the Ra'avad disagrees... A boy jumps up to defend the Rambam... and the boy is fresh. You know how young boys are. He uses improper language so I correct him... we call upon Rabbenu Tam to express his opinion and suddenly a symposium of generations comes into existence....

We... speak one language... chat... laugh... There is *Mesorah* collegiality... comity between old and young... antiquity and Middle Ages and modern times....

I cannot claim my father's Seder produced quite that, but he did give the sense of the characters of the Exodus, and of the rabbis who elaborated on what had happened, as real people, relevant to how I should structure my Seder and my life, from that moment when they told us we have to relive the Seder.

Another such moment came as we moved forward to the blessing before the second cup. Once we had reminded ourselves to celebrate the night as a moment of personal salvation, not celebration of a long-ago event, we said part of

Hallel, praise for the bounty with which God had favored us, and then stood to say the blessing leading in to the second cup of grape juice.

This final blessing celebrates the past and expresses our hope for a return to Israel, the Temple, the sacrificial service. Generally, Jews would have enjoyed two sacrifices Seder night: a *hagigah* offered to serve as the meal leading up to the Paschal sacrifice itself, which was supposed to be eaten while already full, to make clear that the eating is symbolic, not nutritional.

As many Haggadahs note, when Pesach started on Saturday night, we change the word order when referring to those two sacrifices. My father would remind us of that, enthusiastically reviewing why. At a Saturday night Seder, only the Paschal sacrifice would have been offered that day, Shabbat, because only necessary sacrifices were offered on Shabbat. The *hagigah* did not make the cut—in such a year, it would have been offered and eaten sometime during the week after the Seder. Instead of mentioning the זבחים and then the פסחים, the sacrifices and Pesach offerings, we would say על הפסחים ועל הזבחים, the Pesach first, since that is what we would eat first.

That brief annual conversation communicated how firm our family was in our hope to return to such sacrifices. Obvious to many—since traditional texts link that hope to the hope for the Messiah—in adulthood I encountered others, including Orthodox Jews, for whom that was not a hope, let alone belief or expectation.

It started back there, standing at the Seder, cup in hand as we recited this blessing, my father making the Temple as much a part of our lives and our Seder as any other part. In two seconds, in a way that made the lesson stick, despite my fatigue and hunger.

After more than an hour and a half of being taunted by the second cup of grape juice, could life offer anything more sweet than finally drinking it? It took more than a little force of will to resist downing it in one gulp, but the imminence of *matzah*, the knowledge that there was real food right around the corner, helped me stick to my father's two-swallows regimen.

Some complain that Seder *matzah* is flat, dry, and tastes like cardboard, but my family liked it. Even in times of financial stress, we always bought more than just the minimal amount of "hand *shmurah*," the more expensive *matzah* made by hand specifically for the Seder, usually enough to be able to eat that kind of *matzah* throughout the holiday. We tried "machine *shmurah*" one year, but it didn't go.

We ate leaning to the left, in silence, my father chewing slowly and methodically, working his way through unhurriedly, yet faster than any of the rest of us. He'd be preparing the *maror*, the bitter herb, before the second-place person (me, of course) was three quarters of the way through.

Maror was and is a big mystery to me; as per Talmudic prescription, we used romaine lettuce. When I was growing up, iceberg was the salad lettuce, but romaine was by no means unheard of in our home (and does not seem to have the aftertaste the Gemara ascribed to it), and it continues to strike me as an odd choice for a bitter herb.

To some extent, I suspect, that was why my father put grated horseradish inside his romaine when we got to *korech*, the Hillel sandwich. There was also the element of tradition, since that's what his father had used as *maror* (without the romaine to cover it; just *matzah* and raw horseradish, no sugar or beets to soften the taste). The first time I tried it, after he passed away, I put on too much and was taught a lesson in how bitter it could be.

What attracted me to the Hillel sandwich wasn't its being a sandwich, much as I loved sandwiches enough to eat a PB&J every school day of my elementary and almost all of my high school years.

No, I liked the Hillel sandwich because of the little introduction before we eat it: "In memory of the Temple, like Hillel; thus would Hillel do in the time of the Temple, he would combine *matzah* and *maror* (or, more likely, Pesach, *matzah*, and *maror*), to fulfill the verse, על מצות ומררים יאכלהו, with *matzah* and *maror* they should eat it."

Hillel of the long ago past, the hero of Talmudic stories about his patience even with those who baited him, about his dedication to Torah study, whose House became the backbone of accepted Jewish law, that same Hillel I studied in school, was *right there* at my father's Seder, shaping how we experienced *matzah* and *maror*.

As he'd been doing for thousands of years, at my father's Seder, at his father's Seder, at his father's Seder, and so on and so on and so on.

Great, but now it was time to eat.

The Denouement

The two hours of Seder were also an ordinary holiday meal, a story of its own in my family. Here, though, we're paying attention to the Seder, not the day to day pleasures of growing up in my parents' home, sitting at their Shabbat and holiday table. I leave that memoir for another time and, probably, another author.

We cleared away the grape-juice filled saucers under the cups, wiped the many *matzah* crumbs, and set the table for the meal. All while watching for when my father went to the bathroom, since that was the time to steal the *afikoman*.

When he returned, the *afikoman* safely stashed, we started with egg in saltwater, in memory—and a hint of mourning for—the sacrifices in the Temple (the egg on the Seder plate is for similar reasons). I ate the egg because I liked the taste.

My Haggadah would always say that the meal, too, should be dedicated to speaking of the Exodus. After all, people who had in reality just left Egypt would speak only of the momentous events they'd witnessed and lived through. If we successfully re-inserted ourselves into that frame of mind, our meal, too, would be filled with Exodus talk.

At my father's Seder, there was another reason I'd have thought the meal would be filled with Haggadah or Exodus talk. In most years, there had been points in the story where my father had told me or a sibling the hour was late, we'd have to delay discussion of that for the meal.

We rarely got back to it. Meals were too woven into the family fabric to subordinate to the Seder; once in meal mode, the conversation turned as it always did, to our lives, world events, any other occurrences of interest or note. We worked our way through soup with *matzah* balls, fricasseed chicken (a Seder night staple, since my father's custom was not to eat anything roasted, lest it look like a recreation of the Paschal sacrifice). I was no big fan of fricasseed chicken, and Seder night there wasn't even rice, which Ashkenazic custom avoids on Pesach for its looking too much like grains that can leaven.

Aside from the actual dessert, there was *afikoman*, which my father made no effort to eat by the middle of the night (halfway between the start and end of night, not to be confused with midnight—although during the years the clock had not yet changed, it was pretty close). We started this journey with a tale of my father's *afikoman*, but it was enough of a highlight to deserve mention again, the epitome of his concern with our enjoyment, engagement, and attachment to the Seder and the messages it conveyed.

Grace After Meals, *bentching*, was another year-round ritual that slipped into its usual pattern on Seder night. With one significant difference. Leading into *bentching* on Shabbat and holidays, Ashkenazic Jews sing Psalm 126, a song that envisions the future joy when the Temple will be rebuilt. It was special for us on Pesach.

See, in my father's house, we had one tune to that Psalm we could carry reasonably well. The Jews of Hamburg, whence my grandmother hailed, were more musically talented or daring, and had distinct tunes for different occasions—there was a Hamburger Rosh Hashanah tune, Sukkot tune, and other tunes for the different holidays. My father's family had lost all of those except this one, which happened to be the tune for Pesach.

As we started the song Seder night, and for the rest of the holiday, we always said, "The Hamburger Pesach *niggun!*"

By now it was late because the meal expanded or contracted to fill any time the story part had left until it was late. Those years where we got to *matzah* by 10:30, the meal was longer; if we didn't get there until 11:00, the meal was shorter. Either way, we were *bentching* and then saying *Hallel* around the same time.

If there was a young enough child at the table, we might sing *bentching*, and that would help keep us awake, and then we'd sing as much of *Hallel* as we could.

But eventually, we'd get to the part where there's not so much singing, which seemed really long to me as a child, but now, realistically, is five minutes. It might have been longer when the words were less familiar; it certainly felt longer, especially since my father's eyes were sometimes closing as he tried to say the words. It felt like a long pause, punctuated only by the sound of his murmurings while I picked my way through words I didn't yet know from the Shabbat morning liturgy.

It wasn't like I could fake it, either. One of my earliest memories of prayers came from when we still lived in Los

Angeles. I had learned how to read Hebrew and English at a young age, and my father had begun the process of teaching me to pray. He had assigned me what seemed a sizable amount of words, which were all that stood between me and going outside to play with other kids.

I think I was five (we lived in California for two years, but this was early on in my *shul*-going adventures), and I certainly cared more about playing with friends than paying good attention to my conversation with God. The men around me, as far as I could tell, took their fingers and ran it down the page as quickly as they could, saying "mmm mmm MMM mm," or "eheheheheheh."

That seemed like a good solution, because I could go *much* faster that way. And so I did. My father wasn't pleased, and my insistence that that's what all the others were doing didn't wash. For two reasons: he didn't care about what other people did (except for when he did, but mostly he didn't), and in this case, he wanted me to learn the importance of the actual words.

Good lessons, both, but not what I wanted to hear those mornings.

We did eventually get through it, then recited *Nirtzah*, the end of the Seder. Except that it wasn't actually the end, because the songs printed after that were also a highlight, perhaps because they were always a marker of having made it through the whole Seder—an achievement for the very young, adolescent, middle-aged, and elderly. By this point, my father was more than tired enough that he'd prefer to be in bed, but we liked the singing, so he joined us.

He would sing the songs often with eyes closed, sometimes dozing off in the middle. He would sing them with the German accent of his ancestors because I enjoyed it, would make this or that point about the words and the printing, but mostly it was just singing.

Closing with *Chad Gadya*, the song about a baby goat (a kid) that a father bought for two bits, which was eaten by a cat, which was bitten by a dog, and so on, until Hashem kills the Angel of Death. Aside from being last, *Chad Gadya* was the song that had two tunes, the one we all learned at school and knew well, and the one my father's family had sung. We would sing it once to the familiar tune, and then to his tune.

A tradition his children have passed on to their children, remembering the father who bought his children's engagement in his faith with more than two bits, who bought it with years of dedicated involvement, especially but not only on Seder night, combining an insistence on standards, discipline, and effort, with fun, humor, and accommodation to our personal needs that left a lasting foundation, the basis of the faith I pass on to my children, and, hopefully now, to you the reader, in the hope that we all have Seders that include my father's voice, showing us a path to a relationship with God, grounded in the past, fully aware of the present, and excited about what the future may bring.

תם ונשלם שבח לא-ל בורא עולם